AF823115

RURAL BANKING IN INDIA

By

Dr. M. Lakshmi Narasaiah

M.A., Ph.D,
Professor Head
Department of Economics
Sri Krishnadevaraya University Post-graduate Centre
Kurnool-518002
A.P.

DISCOVERY PUBLISHING HOUSE
NEW DELHI-110002

First Published-2003
Reprinted-2010

ISBN 81-7141-635-7

© Author

Published by
DISCOVERY PUBLISHING HOUSE
4831/24, Ansari Road, Prahlad Street,
Darya Ganj, New Delhi-110002 (India)
Phone: 3279245 • Fax: 91-11-3253475
E-mail:dphtemp@indiatimes.com

Printed at: **Mehra Offset Press**

Contents

Preface

The main reason for the backwardness of the rural people in India is the indebtedness of the farmers. The farmer borrows for his agricultural operations, for supporting his family, to make improvements on his land etc. There is nothing wrong in borrowing especially when the funds are required for productive purposes. Every loan is a debt and when the borrower does not repay the loan promptly and goes on accumulating it, he becomes indebted. Indebtedness arises when the income of the farmer is not sufficient to repay the debt he incurred or when he spends his income wastefully, and does not save for the purpose of paying off his debt. The cultivator, when once he runs into debt, is unable to get rid of it. In fact, the farmers borrow year after year, but they are not in a position to pay their debt. Therefore, the debt of the farmer goes on increasing. This is collectively known as rural indebtedness. There is a well known saying which is a truism in our country: "The Indian rural people particularly Indian farmer is born in debt, lives in debt, and dies in debt."

Since the dawn of planning era in India, one of the primary objectives of the Government has been to streamline and strengthen its rural economy and to uplift standards of living of the weaker sections. For the fulfillment of this objective, apart from other agencies, banking institutions are expected to play a dynamic role. Despite the combined efforts of the co-operatives and the commercial banks, the degree of institutionalisation of rural credit was around 30 per cent in the period of 1970s. It is unevenly distributed among different size-group of farmers and strata of rural society. The need for an institutional agency which could combine the rural co-operatives and the business skill of commercial banks was increasingly felt.

The rural people have been depending upon the non-institutional credit sources which have been exploiting them in several ways. This could only be avoided by providing institutional credit. Provisions of institutional finance 'no doubt' will play an important role in bringing about socio-economic changes among the weaker sections.

M.L. Narasaiah

Chapter—1

Introduction

Rural sector plays a significant role in Indian economy. It affects directly or indirectly almost all the economic activities in the country. It employs the maximum number of people. It is also the most important source of national income in India. It also supplies food for the survival of the entire population of India. It also supplies materials necessary for the major industries of India. A large part of the revenue of the Government is also obtained from rural sector. In short, rural sector can be rightly considered as the backbone of our economy. Inspite of significant role of the rural sector, rural sector continues to be neglected. The magnitude of poverty, illiteracy, and ill health is of higher order in the rural areas as compared to the urban areas.

Majority of the rural folk are not able to meet their day-to-day requirements from their own sources of income not to speak of investing in other productive enterprises for improving their economic conditions. Therefore they have to depend on various financial agencies for getting funds for making investment. To bring about the overall development in the rural areas, financial assistance to the rural poor particularly institutional assistance for the development of agriculture needs no emphasis. Finance is an essential requirement for almost every activity. If required finance is not available out of ones own income them one needs credit. In rural areas of India, credit requirements are more pressing. Rural credit in India is a part and parcel of its economic development. Rural population is composed of agricultural producers, tenant cultivators, village artisans and landless labour. All these categories are in need of credit.

The credit requirements of Indian farmers are met by the moneylenders, traders, commission agents, landlords, relatives and the organised institutional agencies like Co-operatives, Commercial Banks, Land Development Banks and Government. Co-operatives have been a major source of rural credit since a very long time. The All India Rural Credit Survey Committee in 1951-52 observed that it fell short of the right quality was not of the right type, did not serve the right purpose and often failed to go to the right people. After nationalisation of 14 Major Commercial Banks, Commercial Banks have also entered into the field and a part of rural credit is met by the different Commercial. Banks. It was felt that the institutional finance was not available to all sections in the rural areas. "The Co-operatives and Commercial Banks are unable to meet all the planned credit requirements of the rural areas".[1] There is a widely shared view the a determined effort is needed to speed up the flow of institutional credit to the weaker sections of the rural community.

The Government of India also felt that it was necessary to establish new institutions, on the basis of attitudinal and operational ethos, entirely different from those obtaining in the nationalised banks.

"The Banking Commission in its report in the year 1972 mooted for the first time the proposal for setting up of rural banks after examining the record of the expansion of the commercial banks activities".[2] A working group appointed by the Government of India, under the Chairmanship of M. Narasimham, examined the problem for rural finance at length and suggested the setting up of Regional Rural Banks. The working group submitted its report within one month and the Government of India accepted the recommendations. The

Regional Rural Banks came into existence with an ordinance in 1975 and subsequently the ordinance was repealed by the Regional Rural Banks Act of 1976. This innovation in the fields of rural credit has added a new dimension to the banking in India. The main objective of the Regional Rural Banks is to provide credit and other facilities for the purpose of development of agriculture, trade, commerce, industry and other productive activities in rural areas. Particularly of the small and marginal farmers, agricultural labourers, artisans and small entrepreneurs.[3]

The Reserve Bank of India in its report has described the setting up of the Regional Rural Banks as a "development which will have far reaching effects on the extension of banking facilities to the rural areas".[4] These new institutions are combining the local feel and familiarity with rural problems which co-operatives possess and the abilities of commercial banks to mobilise the deposits. The major objective of the Regional Rural Banks should not only be to mobilise resources from the region and use them within the same region but also to spread banking in all rural areas for developing banking habit in the countryside. However the idea of new rural banking and the operation of such banks with local staff in rural environment is making the poor people in the villages to feel homely.

STATEMENT OF THE PROBLEM

India, continues to be primarily a rural India with still nearly 70 per cent of its population, seeking employment and living in the rural sector. Since the rural people are unable to meet their credit requirements from their own sources there is a need for providing timely and adequate institutional credit to improve their economic conditions to help especially weaker sections Regional Rural Banks came into existence. The small and marginal farmers and rural artisans find it difficult to make investment on modern inputs like high yielding varieties of seeds, chemical fertilisers, purchase or raw materials, and improved machinery, as they do not have sufficient funds of their own for investment purpose. Hence, Grameena Banks have to extend credit for investment.

Nearly 19 years period is over ever since Regional Rural Banks are set up in different parts of India. It is necessary to examine in depth the functioning of different Regional Rural Banks so as to identify the problems if any, in the effective functioning of the Regional Rural Banks. This study is only an attempt in this direction with special reference to Sree Anantha Grameena Bank in Rayalaseema Region of Andhra Pradesh.

REVIEW OF LITERATURE

In this context, it is necessary to mention the contribution made by a few people with reference to the working of Regional Rural Banks. Mohan Rao (1980) in a case study of Regional Rural Banks with reference to Vishakhapatnam district concluded that the impact of Grameena Bank, on asset building was quite significant through certain categories of target groups have not recorded a considerable increase in asset value.

C. D. Wadhada has made a noteworthy study, entitled "Rural Banks for Rural Development". (1980) This study covered an analysis of the progress made by all Regional Rural Banks in India and offered valuable suggestions for the restructuring of the Regional Rural Banks. This study was conducted in 1977 when the Regional Rural Banks were in the initial stages; and the assessment of their performance was premature.

The Dantwala Committee, after reviewing the performance of the Regional Rural Banks, has concluded that "within a short span of 2 years, the Regional Rural Banks have demonstrated their capability to serve the purpose for which they were established".[5]

E. Nagabhusana Rao and B. Krishnamurty too examined the impact of Regional Rural Banks in achieving the desired goal that is Rural Development.[6] They have mainly analysed the data pertaining to progress made by the beneficiaries. The study is based on both Primary and Secondary sources of information. Most of the studies conducted by the Expert Committees and individual scholars, based on the secondary data, reveals that there is a tremendous progress.

The Sivaraman Committee[7] has rightly pointed out that the progress of the Regional Rural Banks cannot be judged merely based on the growth of deposits and the increase in advances. This clearly shows the need for conducting grassroot level studies to bring out the facts pertaining to its usefulness.

J. S. Garj, G. N. Singh and R. N. Tripati from their study[8] on agriculture financing by Regional Rural Banks concluded that the small and marginal framers are the major beneficiaries. It was also noted that the benefits derived by agricultural labourers are relatively low. The analysis of the purpose wise advances revealed that there was an increasing demand for term-loans, particularly for the development of irrigation, dairying, and poultry. The study was conducted in 1977 when Regional Rural Banks were in the initial stages and hence any assessment of their performance at that stage could not be fairly accurate.

Suresh Kumar[9] had examined the extent of utilisation and impact of credit provided by the Rayalaseema Grameena Bank (Cuddapah); this study was mostly based on the secondary sources of information.

In a study relating to Champaran Kshatriya Grameena Bank in Bihar State, R N. Srivastava (1981)[10] concluded that the Regional Rural Banks provided easy and timely crop-loan at normal rate of interest and such facility resulted in increased use of inputs like seeds, fertilisers, labour and in that way increased intensity of cropping and thereby significantly increased the income of the borrowers.

P. Ramappa,[11] study focussed on the problems of overdues of Sree Anantha Grameena Bank. He analysed the reasons for the overdues in Sree Anantha Grameena Bank and made suggestions to overcome the problem.

Radha Raman Singh,[12] in his Research Paper dealt with the role and says that the NABARD has to pay attention for the development of Regional Rural Banks.

In another study Satya Sundaram 1982[13] concluded the Regional Rural Banks would prove to be more helpful to the rural poor if they pay adequate attention to identify the economically viable products and supervise the end-use of credit by taking services of other local agencies engaged in serving the poor.

The Khelker Committee on Regional Rural Banks 1985[14], appointed by Government of India to assess the working of Regional Rural Banks, found that the authorised share capital and the paid-up capital are inadequate. It is suggested that the share capital is to be subscribed by NABARD instead of by the State Government.

Sujana Kumaris[15] study is also on the working of Sree Anantha Grameena Bank in Anantapur district. She studied the problem of non-agricultural credit supplied by Sree Anantha Grameena Bank. Her study was mainly based upon the information furnished by the Sree Anantha Grameena Bank Office.

The study conducted by C. S. Adhikari[16] mainly refers to the utilisation of Bank Credit under Integrated Rural Development Programme. One of the important findings of the study is most of the programmes are implemented for the sake of fulfilling the targets and have not assessed the relative advantages and disadvantages.

Jagadish Prasad and Sunil Kumar[17] have conducted an empirical study to examine the impact of finance extended on the income levels of the beneficiaries.

The problems of Regional Rural Banks are analysed by A.B.K. Hebbar.[18] The author has pointed out certain constraints in the effective functioning of Regional Rural Banks. The main focus of the research paper is on how to make the Regional Rural Banks functionally efficient.

Balaji[19] made an attempt to evaluate the working of Sree Anantha Grameena Bank. In his study, he mainly dealt with the problems encountered by the beneficiaries, credit deployment and outstanding loans.

The research article by Dr. Nadeem Mohsin and Raghunath Jha[20] deals with the role of Regional Rural Banks in financing the I.R.D.P., the reasons for non-repayment are analysed by the author.

The study conducted by Vasan Anand Kumar[21] exhibits the facts that the weaker sections were availing finance to a low extent compared to upper-caste people.

The study conducted by G. Savaraiah and Nirmalamani[22] refers to the finance extended by Commercial Banks under the Lead Bank Scheme. The study analysed the credit development in the district based on a sample study.

Balishter's[23] article deals with the issue of overdues. One of the important findings of the study is that the farmers are clearing the loans taken from private agencies due to pressure from the money-lenders and also escalation of interest amount in the event of delay. The reason for wilful defaulter is mainly because of the view that loans will be written off and also banks are not institutions for timely repayment. In the light of the study, the author made a few suggestions to overcome such peculiar problems.

K. S. Ramola and K. S. Negi have made an attempt to examine the growth and development of Regional Rural Banks. The paper is mainly based upon official information and lacks empirical support from the farmer's point of view.

The R.K. Agarwal has studied the working and operation of the Prathama Bank in Moradabad and Rampur Districts. His study was based upon the secondary data collected from the concerned Bank and other Banks.

REFERENCE

1. Reserve Bank of India *"Report of the Review Committee on Regional Rural Banks"*, Bombay, 1981 p. 1.
2. *"Report of Banking Commission, New Delhi, Government of India"*, 1972 p. 165-174.
3. *Ibid* p. 5.
4. *Reserve Bank of India Report on Currency and Finance 1975-76*, Vol. I 'Economic Review', Bombay, 1976 p. 100.

5. *Ibid* p. 74.
6. E. Nagabhusana Rao and B. Krishnamurty. *"Five Years of Regional Rural Banks"*, Kurukshetra, Vol. XXIX No. 8 January 16, 1981 p. 17.
7. B. Sivaraman, *"The Arrangements for Institutional Credit for Agriculture and Rural Development.* "Reserve Bank of India Report", March 30, 1979.
8. J. S. Garg etc., *"An Analysis of Agricultural Financing by Regional Rural Banks in Moradabad District of Uttar Pradesh"*. Journal of Agricultural Economics, Vol. 23, No. 24, 1958 p. 31-36.
9. D. V. Suresh Kumar, *"Functioning of Regional Rural Banks"*, M. Phil., Thesis, S. K. University, Anantapur, 1982.
10. R. N. Srivastava, *"Impact of Champaran Kshtriya Grameena Bank on Rural Economy"*, Economic Affairs, Vol. 26 (4), 1981 p. 266-272.
11. P. Ramappa, *"A Study of Overdues in Regional Rural Banks"*, M. Phil., thesis, S. K. University, Anantapur.
12. Radha Raman Singh, *"Regional Rural Banks and the Rural Poor"*, Kurukshetra, Vol. XXXI, No. 11 February, 16, 1983 p. 22.
13. I. Satya Sundaram, *"Problems Facing by Regional Rural Banks"*, Paper presented at the Seminar on *"Changing Trends in Development Banking"*, conducted by the Department of Commerce, Andhra University, Waltair, 1982.
14. All India Committee on Regional Rural Banks, 1985.
15. J. Sujana Kumari, *"The Role of Sree Anantha Grameena Bank in a Drought Prone District* (with special reference to non-agricultural loans). Unpublished M. Phil., thesis, S. K. University, Anantapur, 1984.
16. Adhikari, C. S. *"Credit Disbursement and Percolation of Benefits under I.R.D.P.*, Kurukshetra, Vol. XXXIII, No. 7, April, 1985, pp. 20-23-28.
17. Jagadish Prasad and Sunil Kumar, *"Regional Rural Banks, An Evaluation of Performance,* Southern Economist", 21 (6), 15 July, 1982.
18. Hebbar, *"Problems of Regional Rural Banks, Kurukshetra, April 1985"*, Vol. 33 No. 7, pp. 22-24 and 30.
19. Balaji, *"Performance Evaluation of Sree Anantha Grameena Bank"*, Unpublished M. Phil., Thesis, S.K. University. 1985.

20. Dr. Nadeem Mohsin and Raghunatha Jha, *"Regional Rural Banks and I.R.D.P.,"* Yojana, July 16-31, 1987 pp. 10-13.

21. Vasan Anand Kumar, *"Performance of Regional Rural Banks"*, Kurukshetra. Vol. XXXXI No. 8, May, 1988 p. 16.

22. Savaraiah and Nirmalamani, *Role of Lead Bank: A Case Study*. Yojana, Vol. 33 No. 6, April 1-15, 1989 pp. 32-34.

23. Balishter, *Agricultural Loans: Meanance of Overdues*. Yojana, July 16-31, 1989, pp. 30-33.

Chapter—2

Genesis and Growth of Regional Rural Banks in India

One of the main reasons for the backwardness of the rural people in India is the indebtedness of the farmers. The farmer borrows for his agricultural operations, for supporting his family, to make improvements on his land etc. There is nothing wrong in borrowing especially when the funds are required for productive purposes. Every loan is a debt when the borrower does not repay the loan promptly and goes on accumulating it, he becomes indebted. Indebtedness arises when the income of the farmers is not sufficient to repay the debt he incurred or when he spends his income wastefully, and does not save for the purpose of paying off his debt. The cultivator, when once he runs into debt, is unable to get rid of it. Infact, the Indian farmers borrows year after year, but they are not in a position to pay their debt. Therefore the debt to the farmer goes on increasing. This is collectively known as rural indebtedness. There is a well known saying which is a truism in our country; "The Indian Rural people particularly Indian farmer is born in debt, lives in debt, and dies in debt."

Since the dawn of planning era in India, one of the primary objectives of the Government has been to streamline and strengthen its rural economy and to uplift standards of living of the weaker sections. For the fulfilment of this objective, apart from other agencies, Banking institutions are expected to play a dynamic role. Despite the combined efforts of the Co-operatives and the Commercial Banks, the degree of institutionalisation of rural credit was around 30 per cent by the Nineteen Seventees. It is unevenly distributed among the different size-groups of farmers and strata of rural society. The need for an institutional agency which could combine the rural co-operatives and the business skill of Commercial Banks was increasingly felt.

The rural people have been depending upon the non-institutional credit sources which have been exploiting them in several ways. This could only be avoided by providing institutional credit. Provisions of institutional finance 'no doubt' will play an important role in bringing about socio-economic changes among the rural population. In the absence of adequate and timely credit facilities from the institutions, private agencies dominate naturally rural credit scene. The nationalisation of major Commercial Banks in 1969 and 1980 resulted in the tremendous progress in purveying institutional finance to the rural areas. However, it is noticed the Commercial Banks extended benefits mostly to the richer sections of the rural areas. Moroever, the savings mobilised from the rural areas have flown into urban and metropolitan areas and not to meet the needs of the weaker sections of the rural community[1]. Therefore, there is a widely shared view that a more determined effort was needed to speed-up the flow of institutional credit, especially to meet the needs of the weaker sections of the rural community.[2]

Government of India appointed a working group on July 1, 1975 to examine indepth the setting up of new rural banks as subsidiaries of Public Sector Banks to cater the credit needs of the rural poor under the Chairmanship of Sri. M. Narasimham. The group identified various weaknesses of the co-operative agencies and the Commercial Banks and felt the existing institutions, with their present structure, would not be able to fill the regional and functional gap in the institutional credit system. The group also felt that, in a country of the size and regional diversity as ours, no single pattern, be it Commercial Banks or Co-operative credit can be expected to meet all the emerging requirements in all areas. A degree of adaptation and improvisation is called for and the range of institutional alternatives widened. It is in this context that we have come to the conclusion that a new type of institution is necessary. It, therefore, recommended the setting up of the state-sponsored, region based and rural-oriented Commercial Banks, called Regional Rural Banks.

REGIONAL RURAL BANKS ACT—1976

Accepting the recommendations of the working group, the Government of India promulgated the Regional Rural Banks Ordinance on September 26, 1975 and first five Regional Rural Banks were established on October 2, 1975. The Ordinance was later replaced by the Regional Rural Banks Act 1976. The Regional Rural Banks were to be set up mainly "with a view to developing the rural economy by providing credit and other facilities for the purpose of development of agriculture, trade, commerce, industry and other productive activities in the rural areas. Particularly to the small and marginal farmers, agricultural labourers, artisans and small entrepreneurs".[3] The operational area of Regional Rural Banks is relatively small and confining to the specified area. The staff of Regional Rural Banks is expected to be recruited locally. This would mean that the staff is familiar with the local language and environment. The Regional Rural Banks have been evolved as "Low Cost and Rural based institutions and therefore eminently suited to implement bankable schemes in the rural areas."[4] The management of each Regional Rural Bank is to be through the Board of Directors consisting of 9-12 members headed by a Chairman. The Chairman is to be appointed by the Government on India on the recommendations of the sponsor banks. The sponsor banks normally recommend a person from among its own employees for this position and they would be on deputation with the Regional Rural Banks. The Central Government nominates three directors in addition to the Chairman. The State Government nominates two Directors, while the sponsor Bank nominates the remaining three Directors. The Chairman is required to devote his whole time to the affairs of the Regional Rural Banks, subject to the superintendence control and direction of the Board of Directors. He will look after the whole management of the Regional Rural Banks.

Each Regional Rural Bank is expected to cover a population ranging from 5,000 to 2,00,000. Though the Regional Rural Banks were set up with a view to bring out overall development of the rural areas, the main emphasis is on assisting the small farmers in obtaining the required inputs and in extending financial help and other help required by them. With the establishment of Regional Rural Banks the Bank branches were spread to even the remote areas which is again a boon to those who want to avail benefits. The sponsoring bank will also help the Regional Rural Banks in several ways. To start with, the sponsoring bank will met the initial expenditure in the establishment of a Regional rural Bank. It deputes its staff and also arranges for appointment and training of the personnel. Sponsoring Bank is like a guide, friend and philosopher to the Regional Rural Bank. Regional Rural Banks are also provided with insurance coverage for the deposits to the maximum extent of Rs. 30,000 per account.

INCORPORATION AND CAPITAL OF REGIONAL RURAL BANKS

Every Regional Rural Bank shall be a body corporate with perpetual succession and a common seal with power, subject to the provisions of this Act to acquire, hold and dispose of property and to contact and may sue a place in notified areas as the Central Government may decide after consultation with Reserve Bank of India and the sponsor Bank.

The authorised capital of each Regional Rural Bank was placed at Rs. 1.00 crore and issued capital at Rs. 25.00 lakhs. The issued capital would be subscribed by the Government of India. The sponsoring Bank and the concerned State Government at the ratio of 50 per cent, 35 per cent and 15 per cent respectively. The authorised capital of each Regional Rural Bank shall be One

Crore rupees divided into One Lakh of fully paid-up shares of One Hundred rupees each provided that the Central Government may, after consultation with the Reserve Bank of India and the sponsor Bank, increase or decrease such authorised capital and it shall not be reduced below twenty five lakhs of rupees. In the beginning, the Reserve Bank of India provided refinance facilities and this task is now taken by the National Bank for Agricultural and Rural Development (NABARD). The NABARD apart from providing refinance facility undertakes the responsibility of formulation of operational policies, especially of new Regional Rural Banks and oversees their overall functioning.

After making provisions for bad and doubtful debts, depreciation in assets, contribution to the staff and superannuation funds and all other matters which are usually provided for by banking companies, Regional Rural Banks may out of its net profits declare dividend.

Each Regional Rural Bank has the status of a scheduled Commercial Bank and has been empowered to mobilise deposits and to grant short team loans to the small and marginal farmers, agricultural labourers, rural artisans—small entrepreneurs and persons of small means engaged in any productive activity. They also grant loans to all types of co-operative activity. They also grant loans to all types of Co-operative Societies and farmers service societies operating within the area of operation of Regional Rural Banks. The aim behind the starting of Regional Rural Banks is to help the weaker sections to acquire productive assets for the purpose of improving their earning capacity. They also provide loans both for productive and consumption purposes. Though the Regional Rural Banks are Commercial Banks, their objectives and lending procedures are different from those of the ordinary Commercial Banks functioning in the country.

Every Regional Rural Bank is authorised to carry and transact the business of banking as defined in Clause 6 of Section 5 of the Banking Companies Act 1949 and may engage in one or more forms of business specified in Sub-section 1 of Section

6 of that Act without prejudice to the generality of the provisions of Sub-section 1. Every Regional Rural Bank is required to undertake the following types of business: (1) granting loans and advances to small and marginal farmers and agricultural labourers, whether individually or in groups and to co-operative societies or framers service societies for agricultural operations or for both related purposes and (2) granting of loans and advances to artisans, small entrepreneurs and persons of small means engaged in trade, commerce or industry or other productive activities within its area of operations.

It is a well known fact that alongwith the process of planned development in India, imbalances cropped up. The phenomenon of unequal rate of economic growth of various reasons within the country is becoming so pronounced that it is of immence interest to policy makers to fulfil the objectives of balanced regional development by providing necessary credit facilities to the needed population of all regions.

GROWTH OF THE REGIONAL RURAL BANKS

Regional Rural Banks are sponsored by Scheduled Commercial Banks usually Public Sector Commercial Banks. A few non-public sector banks have also sponsored Regional Rural Banks. Following a view taken by the Reserve Bank of India in consultation with the Government of India, Scheduled State Co-operative Banks are also allowed to sponsor Regional Rural Banks.

The Regional Rural Banks were inaugurated on 2nd October 1975. One of the first Regional Rural Banks to be established is the "Prathama Bank" sponsored by the Syndicate Bank in Muradabad district of Uttar Pradesh. On the same day, four other Regional Rural Banks were sponsored by other public sector banks. Since their inception, Regional Rural Banks made rapid strides of progress both in respect of branch expansion and advancement of loans to the weaker sections. Since the inception of these banks, the number of Regional Rural Banks established in the country has gone upto 196 by the end of March 1990. The growth of Regional Rural Banks from 1985 to 1993 is presented in Table—2.1.

PROGRESS OF REGIONAL RURAL BANKS

Table—2.1

Number of Regional Rural Banks and Districts Covered and their No. of Branches, Deposits and Outstanding Advances (As on December, 1993)

Sl. No.	*As on*		*No. of RRBs*	*Districts covered*	*No. of Branches*	*`Deposits*	*Outstand-ing advances*	*C.D. Ratio*
1.	Dec.	'85	188	333	12,686	1,28,582	1,48,767	189
2.	Dec.	'86	194	351	12,838	1,71,494	1,78,484	104
3.	Dec.	'87	196	363	13,353	2,30,582	2,23,226	97
4.	Dec.	'88	196	369	13,920	2,96,588	2,88,429	95
5.	Sept.	'89	196	370	14,279	3,46,799	3,15,493	91
6.	Sept.	'90	196	388	14,511	4,26,752	3,55,517	83
7.	March	'91	196	381	14,527	4,98,924	3,69,927	72
8.	Sept.	'92	196	385	14,531	5,14,133	3,88,368	74
9.	March	'93	196	388	14,531	4,26,752	3,55,517	74

Source: Statistics on Regional Rural Banks, NABARD, March 1993.

From Table—2.1, it is evident that there has been continuous increase in the bank branches of Regional Rural Banks. The deposits and advances have also correspondingly increased. At the end of 1985, there existed only 188 Regional Rural Banks and the figure has increased to 196 in 1993. Thus, between 1985 and 1993, there was a very much increase in the number of branches of Regional Rural Banks. The credit deposit ratio is one of the important indicators in judging the performance of Regional Rural Banks, the ratio has increased to 189., Though it has declined, the C.D. Ratio of Regional Rural Banks is comparatively higher than the Rural branches of well-established Commercial Banks. Hence, there is a need for improving the credit deposit ratio by the Regional Rural Banks.

Table 2.1 presents the number of Regional Rural Banks and the districts covered with branches since their inception to March 1993 as collected and shown in the Table—2.1. The Regional

Rural Banks have shown a tremendous growth in their No. of Branches, deposits and outstanding advances. At the end of March 1993, the No. of districts covered was 388 and the No. of Branches was 14,531. It shows there is a very good growth in Regional Rural Banks.

Table—2.2 presents the state-wise number of the Regional Rural Banks and the districts covered with branches since their inception to March 1993. Uttar Pradesh has the highest number of Regional Rural Banks covering 56 districts with 2,994 branches followed by Madhya Pradesh 24 Banks covering 44 districts with 1,577 branches and Andhra Pradesh 16 Banks covering 23 districts with 1,101 branches. The state of Manipur, Meghalaya, Nagaland, Arunachal Pradesh and Mizoram are the least; they have only single Regional Rural Bank covering their branches in 8 districts, 3 districts, 7 districts, 4 districts and 3 districts respectively. So, it is suggested that the States which are having more districts have to establish some more Regional Rural Banks to improve their branches to cater the bank services in rural areas.

Table—2.2
State-wise Number of Regional Rural Banks and Their Branches (As on March, 1993)

Sl. No.	*Name of the State/ Union Territory*	*No. of RRBs*	*No. of Districts*	*No. of Branches*
	1	**2**	**3**	**4**
1.	Andhra Pradesh	16	23	1,101
2.	Assam	5	20	322
3.	Arunachal Pradesh	1	4	16
4.	Bihar	22	38	1,820
5.	Gujarat	9	17	386
6.	Haryana	4	11	289
7.	Himachal Pradesh	2	4	125
8.	Jammu & Kashmir	3	10	256
9.	Karnataka	13	20	1,059

(Contd. ...)

1		2	3	4
10.	Kerala	2	6	269
11.	Madhya Pradesh	24	44	1,577
12.	Maharashtra	10	17	573
13.	Manipur	1	8	24
14.	Meghalaya	1	3	46
15.	Mizoram	1	3	44
16.	Nagaland	1	7	10
17.	Orissa	9	13	815
18.	Punjab	5	10	158
19.	Rajasthan	14	27	1,056
20.	Tamilnadu	3	7	198
21.	Tripura	1	3	84
22.	Uttar Pradesh	40	56	2,994
23.	West Bengal	9	18	818

Source: Statistics on Regional Rural Banks, NABARD March, 1993.

Table—2.3 shows the distribution of branches of Regional Rural Banks and their deposits and advances among the various regions in India as on September, 1993. The total branches are 14,531 in India and the total deposits Rs. 5,14,132.97 crores. By the end of September 1993, the total advances also increased to Rs. 3,89,369.16 crores. The credit deposit ratio is one of the important indicators in judging the performance of Regional Rural Banks. The ratio has increased to 74 in all over India. The performance of Regional Rural Banks in southern region and western region, whose credit deposit ratio is above 100, is satisfactory. But, the performance of Regional Rural Banks, whose credit deposit ratio is below 100 is not satisfactory. Viewed from this angle, nearly 50 per cent of Regional Rural Banks performance is below the satisfactory level. Hence, there is a need for improving the credit-deposit ratio by the Regional Rural Banks.

The Banking institutions must devote sufficient interest both in the expansion of credit as well as deposit mobilisation with

Table—2.3

Region/State-wise No. of R.R. Bs and their Branches, Deposits, Oustanding Advance (as on September, 1993)

(Deposits Rs. in corores)

Name of the State	*No. of RRBs*	*Districts covered*	*No. of Branches*	*Deposits*	*Agricultural advances*	*Non-Agri-cultural advances*	*Total Advances*	*Over due advances*	*C.D. Ratio*
Northern Region									
Hayrana	4	14	291	18,587.34	5,884.52	7,298.32	13,182.84	5,817.89	7.1
Himachal Pradesh	2	4	129	6,675.78	683.81	1,454.62	2,138.43	684.79	32
Jammu & Kashmir	3	12	268	6,821.61	1,138.59	1,958.57	3,097.16	878.97	45
Punjab	5	10	201	8,968.92	3,791.17	2,387.15	6,898.32	1,381.58	76
Rajasthan	14	28	1868	39,381.84	7,554.81	7,728.81	15,282.82	5,378.27	50
North Eastern Region									
Andhra Pradesh	1	4	19	356.99	50.44	33.85	84.29	29.87	24
Assam	5	23	482	12,887.45	3,748.26	5,567.38	9,315.56	3,852.53	73
Manipur	1	8	29	193.55	189.37	167.98	277.35	168.78	143
Meghalaya	1	3	50	1,701.81	438.41	109.37	547.78	136.96	32
Mizoram	1	3	850	830.16	122.29	346.48	468.77	127.38	56
Nagaland	1	7	8	59.84	21.20	33.41	54.61	34.51	91

the bank branch expansion of Regional Rural Banks deposits will also increase. It is also noticed that Regional Rural Banks have been relatively better in deposit-mobilisation in rural areas compared to co-operative credit societies.

DEVELOPMENT OF CREDIT

The main drive behind setting up of Regional Rural Banks is to extend financial assistance to weaker sections of the rural areas with specific reference to small and marginal farmers, agricultural labourers—rural artisans and small entrepreneurs.

In India, as many as 76.6 per cent of the people are living in rural areas. Since the rural people are unable to meet their credit requirements from their own sources, there is need for providing timely and adequate institutional credit to improve their economic conditions. It is a well known fact that the income levels of the rural people can be increased by raising their capacity to invest in their economic activities. To help specially weaker sections Regional Rural Banks came into existence.

It is important to note that the NABARD has been liberally refinancing the Regional Rural Banks. All the Regional Rural Banks, irrespective of their age of operation, are provided refinance for short-term. Under this scheme, there is no limit for drawal and refinance in a year. Further the refinance will be provided 3 per cent less than the bank rate. The Regional Rural Banks which have five years of operation or more were provided two refinance limits.

Table—2.4 shows the bank-wise borrowings by Regional Rural Banks with sponsor banks, NABARD, I.D.B.I., and others as on 1993 in Andhra Pradesh.

From the Table—2.4, it is clear that the NABARD has been financing the Regional Rural Banks more than sponsor banks and other banks. It has to be emphasised again and again that the NABARD has been providing more financial assistance than other banking institutions. The Rayalaseema Grameena Bank has been taken the highest amount from NABARD than other banks. The Golconda Grameena Bank has been taken the lowest amount from NABARD.

Table—2.4
Bank-wise Borrowings by R.R.Bs with Sponsor Banks, NABARD, IDBI and Others in A.P. as on December, '93

Name of the Bank	*Sponsor Banks*	*From NABARD Non-Schematic*	*NABARD Schematic*	*IDBI/ SIDBI*	*Others*	*Total*
Nagarjuna	881.02	1,254.65	244.29	6.17	1.12	2,387.25
Rayalaseema	1,571.18	4,353.88	933.46	27.96	7.08	6,893.56
Sri Vishakha	815.00	2,007.00	4.00	2.00	602.00	3,430.00
Sree Anantha	301.73	808.98	765.07	33.50	—	1,909.28
Venkateswara	559.14	1,295.77	318.94	9.12	—	2,182.97
Saraswathi	280.02	637.70	283.67	24.77	—	1,226.16
Sangameswara	285.28	826.63	347.98	—	19.79	1,479.68
Manjira	367.00	893.00	592.00	57.00	—	1,909.00
Pinakini	425.86	1,386.08	549.26	2.36	4.60	2,368.16
Kakatiya	200.08	485.38	121.74	60.61	-	867.81
Chaitanya	276.71	738.69	358.71	—	-	1,374.11
Sathavahana	267.77	605.79	219.65	—	—	1,093.21
Golconda	71.96	194.12	74.80	—	—	676.91
Sri Rama	146.48	366.42	79.62	—	84.39	676.91
Kanakadurga	136.33	379.15	—	—	—	515.48
Godavari	118.92	314.31	150.90	—	—	584.13

Source: Statistics on R.R.Bs NABARD (September, 1994)

PROGRESS OF REGIONAL RURAL BANKS IN ANDHRA PRADESH

In Andhra Pradesh, Nagarjuna Grameena Bank was the first Regional Rural Bank established on 30th April 1976 under Regional Rural Banks Act. It covers both Khammam and Nalgonda districts. The Hyderabad district is considered to be urban and is not eligible to be covered by Regional Rural Banks. Out of the remaining 22 districts, were covered by 16 Regional Rural Banks. Table—2.5 presents the overall picture of Regional Rural Banks in Andhra Pradesh as on 1993.

Identification of the right type of borrowers who are really in need of finance is an important issue. Recovery ratio is another problem. Lack of technical staff which hinders the Regional Rural Banks in granting loans to the right persons in right time is another serious problem. Further, the borrowers seem to entertain false impression that the Regional Rural Banks, on par with other institutional agencies, will waive the loans granted to them. This type of thinking results in increasing the magnitude of overdues. It is also stated that the coverage of agricultural laboures and rural artisans is only in records rather than in practice. Identification of borrowers who are really in need of loan and who can honestly repay the loan amount is a crucial problem.

Another aspect of the problem is that Regional Rural Banks are controlled by too many agencies, Reserve Bank of India, NABARD, sponsor bank and State Government which hinders the scope for independent decision making. The success or Regional Rural Banks depends upon the improving credit-deposit ratio; on the other hand, the farmers must be inculcated to the habit of repayment of the loans as scheduled.

Table—2.6 *(See table on page 24)* presents the performance of Regional Rural Banks in Andhra Pradesh as on 1993. The percentage of recovery of Rayalaseema Grameena Bank was very low; the percentage of recovery of Godavari Grameena Bank was very high. The collection amount of Rayalaseema Grameena Bank was very high; the collection amount of Kakatiya

Table—2.5
Date of Establishment and the Name of the Sponsor Bank and Jurisdiction of the R.R.Bs in Andhra Pradesh as at the end of March, 1993

Sl. No.	*Name of the Regional Rural Bank*	*Date of Establishment*	*Name of the Sponsor Bank*	*Jurisdiction of the Bank*
1.	Nagarjuna Grameena Bank	30.04.1976	State Bank of India	Khammam and Nalgonda
2.	Rayalaseema Grameena Bank	06.06.1976	Syndicate Bank	Cuddapah and Kurnool
3.	Sree Vishakha Grameena Bank	31.09.1976	State Bank of India	Srikakulam, Visakhapatnam, Vijayanagaram
4.	Sree Anantha Grameena Bank	01.11.1979	Syndicate Bank	Anantapur
5.	Sree Venkateswara Grameena Bank	22.03.1981	Indian Bank	Chittoor
6.	Sri Saraswathi Grameena Bank	30.03.1982	State Bank of India	Dilabad
7.	Sangameswara Grameena Bank	31.03.1982	State Bank of Hyderabad	Mahaboob Nagar
8.	Manjira Grameena Bank	31.03.1982	State Bank of Hyderabad	Medak
9.	Pinakini Grameena Bank	11.06.1982	Syndicate Bank	Nellore and parts of the Prakasam
10.	Kakatiya Grameena Bank	28.06.1982	State Bank of India	Warangal
11.	Chaitanya Grameena Bank	25.03.1983	Andhra Bank	Guntur
12.	Sree Sathavahana Grameena Bank	28.03.1983	Andhra Bank	Karimnagar
13.	Golkonda Grameena Bank	15.02.1985	State Bank of Hyderabad	Rangareddy
14.	Sree Rama Grameena Bank	21.02.1985	State Bank of Hyderabad	Nizamabad
15.	Kanakadurga Grameena Bank	28.03.1986	Indian Bank	Krishna
16.	Godavari Grameena Bank	11.04.1987	Andhra Bank	East & West Godavari

Source: Based on the Statistics on R.R.Bs as on June, 1993. NABARD

Table—2.6
Performance of R.R.Bs in Andhra Pradesh as on March, 1993

Sl. No.	Name of the Bank	No. of Districts Covered	No. of Staff	No. of Branches	Demand	Collection	Balance	% of Recovery
1.	Sri Rama Grameena Bank	1	168	25	1185.27	875.75	309.52	73.89
2.	Rayalaseema Grameena Bank	3	955	142	8645.00	3505.00	5140.00	40.54
3.	Pinakini Grameena Bank	2	497	83	3089.42	1460.75	1628.67	47.28
4.	Saraswathi Grameena Bank	1	307	71	1899.78	1359.86	539.92	71.58
5.	Majira Grameena Bank	1	331	64	1925.00	1073.00	852.00	55.74
6.	Kakathiya Grameena Bank	1	190	43	1304.00	466.00	838.00	35.74
7.	Venkateswara Grameena Bank	1	425	71	2776.95	1191.67	1585.28	41.91
8.	Golconda Grameena Bank	1	24	24	561.85	173.59	388.26	30.90
9.	Nagarjuna Grameena Bank	2	148	148	1453.69	921.33	532.36	63.38
10.	Vishakha Grameena Bank	3	168	168	4012.00	1752.00	2260.00	43.67
11.	Anantha Grameena Bank	1	422	70	2335.73	1063.70	1272.03	45.54
12.	Sathavahana Grameena Bank	1	203	46	1475.51	718.26	757.25	48.68
13.	Chaitanya Grameena Bank	1	238	45	2758.97	1331.88	1427.09	48.27
14.	Sangameswara Grameena Bank	1	294	65	1656.76	844.15	812.61	50.95
15.	Godavari Grameena Bank	2	131	37	769.68	635.23	134.45	82.53
16.	Kanakadurga Grameena Bank	1	111	27	802.19	696.13	106.06	86.78

Source: Statistics on Regional Rural Banks, R.R.Bs Division, NABARD 1994.

Grameena Bank was very low. The performance of Regional Rural Banks, by and large, seems to be encouraging. Yet, they have to render greater service in view of growing credit requirement of the rural poor.

PROBLEMS

Although the progress of the Regional Rural Banks is commendable, still there are certain gaps in their functioning. It is found that the credit channelised through the institutional agencies is less than the requirement. Inspite of widespread bank expansion, still there are underbanked areas. The gap between the demand and supply of the credit from existing institutional agencies is wide. While the co-operatives are democratic institutions, the Commercial Banks, and even the Regional Rural Banks are bureaucratic institutions. They are not likely to succeed in enticing the co-operation of the Rural Public and commanding their support and participation.

Since the Regional Rural Banks are satisfying to a large extent all the conditions of a sound rural credit system in the context of problem hidden area, it is desirable to take necessary steps by the Government of India for their expansion in a large scale. All the primary agricultural co-operative credit societies and the rural branches of Commercial Banks may be brought under the fold of Regional Rural Banks at an early date to avoid unnecessary competition, inefficiency and to have sound credit system all over the country. For each district, one Regional Rural Bank may be designed with sufficient number of branches, depending upon the size and needs of the district.

REFERENCE

1. Reserve Bank of India, *"Regional Rural Banks"*, p. 4.
2. *Ibid.*, page No. 4.
3. *Ibid.*, p. 6.
4. L.D. Mello, *"Lead Bank Scheme and Role of Banks"*, S.B.I. Economic Review", February 1976, p. 68.

Chapter—3

Bank Finance—its Structure, Growth, Performance for Rural Development

In order to stimulate the development of Banking and to give sustained support to the development of Co-operative Banks, and other Co-operative institutions by providing remittances and other facilities, the All India Rural Credit Survey Committee recommended the Government of India to set up of Public Sector Bank which would be responsive to the needs of the rural sector in general and Co-operative institutions in particular. However, Co-operative credit could not be developed uniformly in all parts of the country. Further, All India Rural Credit Survey Committee observed that "perhaps the most startling revelation of survey has been the utter insignificance of the volume of credit supplied to the cultivator by the co-operative movement, co-operative agricultural credit is in quantitative terms little more than three per cent of the borrowings of the cultivator... . What reaches the medium and small cultivator from the co-operative institutions is a mere fraction of the little that co-operatives provide".[1] Rural credit and poverty alleviation have thus become inextricably linked over past three decades. The rural development is merely a programme to reduce the pressure on the poor from the clutches of the informal money-lenders. The All India Rural Credit Survey (AIRCS), published by the Committee of Direction in 1954, revealed the high degree of 88 per cent of rural poor depending on higher non-institutional credit. Inadequate supply of institutional credit was identified as a major constraint on increasing productivity. The State Bank of India established a division of Rural Branches in 1995, as the co-operatives could not rise up to the expectations and demand. The number of rural branches of Commercial Banks grew thereafter from 1832 in 1969. The Committee identified the lack of collateral as a handicap for rural households attaining credit and suggested that Banks should base their credit worthiness on the expected returns to the investment rather than on the assets of households.

In 1977, the All India Rural Credit Review Committee (AIRCRC) revealed some improvement in institutional credit from 1951-71 for cultivator-households, but the situation for non-cultivators worsened despite the spread of Banking infrastructure. Share of debt owed to institutional sources increased from 12 per cent (1951) to 31.5 per cent (1971) for cultivator-households, but for non-cultivator households share of debt owed, money-lenders' relatives, friends and other sources increased from 88 per cent to 90 per cent during the period. Forty per cent of rural households (78 million) fell into the category of non-cultivators and had assets less than Rs. 2500 in 1971. Even money-lenders were generally unwilling to provide medium or long-term credit to this group except in exchange for equally long labour contracts. Primary Agricultural Co-operatives were tailored to cultivators/demand for short-term crop finance. Other programmes such as Small Farmers Development Agency/Marginal Farmers Agricultural Labour/ SFDA/MFAL were launched in the 70's to overcome productivity constraints. In general, programmes continued to benefit rural households with land of other collateral.

There was a marked difference between these agencies (SFDA/MFAL) which emphasized facilitating rural growth through credit and technology adoption and a new view, also emerging in the early 1970's of growth with social justice through credit. By this new strategy, adherents of the latter strategy in academic and Government began to see Banks not simply as profit maximizers channelling investment to the most productive uses, but as underutilized institutions to be activated for affirmative action social engineering, and redistribution of wealth. This change in perception was first manifested by the Differential Interest Rates (DIR) scheme foisted upon newly nationalized Commercial Banks in 1971. Under DIR, Public Sector Banks were instructed to channel atleast part of their outstanding advances in productive ventures of families with income and land-holdings below a certain threshold. Many Banks saw DIR-lending with its highly subsidized interest rates and overdues, generally exceeding 50 per cent, as the social cost as doing business and seldom exerted themselves on recovery. The DIR scheme entertained instead of the traditional view that Banks should earn a net positive return of individual loans, a different view in favour of gross subsidization as a priority to rural credit. Although the interest rates on IRDP was greater than DIR (10 per cent vs 4 per cent), it offered beneficiaries not only below interest rates, but also capital subsidies a new variant on rural interest.

Another new institution, the Regional Rural Bank (RRB) was established in 1975 to augment the supply of credit and provide a low cost debt to rural branches of Commercial Banks that would lend exclusively to the poor using simplified procedure. The Banking Commission which recommended their formation in 1972 called for 49 per cent local membership of RRB's and 51 per cent by sponsoring Commercial Banks, thus combining the membership-cum-responsibility strengths of cooperativism with the efficiency of Commercial Banks. The Government ignored this critical dimension, consisting 50 per cent ownership of the Regional Rural Banks to the Central Government, 35 per cent sponsor Banks, and 15 per cent to State Governments. No equality remained for local borrowers/depositors—a factor that may continue to negatively affect appraisal standards and repayment-ethics in these institutions. Strict directives by the

Ministry of Finance are likely to worsen the situation since Central Government ownership through the National Bank for Agriculture and Rural Development (NABARD) has been increased 60 per cent and the Central government's share 20 per cent. Commercial Banks are certain to increase the drain on their profitable operations arising from below-interest rates. Low recoveries of RRBs may diminish as a result of this change which reduces their stake from 35 per cent to 20 per cent. Financial discipline in lending to the poor can be expected to deteriorate further. This will increasingly be viewed as an arm of Government rather than interdependent institutions which are subject to the consequences of their own concessions.

The 1981 Report of the Committee to Review Arrangements for Institutional Credit for Agriculture and Rural Development (CRAFICARD) noted the profound shift in perception of Banks' social role. It stated that in order to foster growth with social justice, credit must be available to the poor. Appraisal standards for the poor ought to shift their emphasis on collateral toward assessment to the viability of the department itself. Although co-operative credit institutions had been urged to accept this concept more than two decades earlier, institutional credit continued to discriminate against the assetless poor by requiring collateral or third party guarantees for most loans. CRAFICARD traced the basic cause of poverty to the low resource-base of the rural poor, their continued heavy dependence on non-institutional credit for consumption finance, and lack of access to medium and long-term finance for productive investment. It postulated that poor, if given access to credit for investment in productive assets (physical and skills) would increase their income through self-employment.

Committee to Review Arrangement for Institutional Credit for Agricultural and Rural Development provided the conceptual underpinning for expanding IRDP. Yet many of its key recommendations were not incorporated in to the programme. It envisaged a household approach to poverty eradication spearheaded by Banks that would classify poor households into three groups. Those who could be made viable with loan assistance; those who would need loan plus a capital-subsidy to become viable; and the non-viable poor who require special assistance in the form of social scrutiny. CRAFICARD's target group were small and marginal farmers, agricultural labourers, rural artisans and SCs/STs. IRDP did not adopt an income standard for eligibility but provided no means to separate out those who could become 'viable' through credit. The committee noted that new delivery mechanisms were necessary to supply the poor with credit because dispersion and small loan size raised transaction costs. Organizing poor households into functional groups would help Banks to achieve economies of scale, thus improving the efficiency of such operations. Ignoring this dimension, Integrated Rural Development Programme (IRDP) planners continued to focus on the lack of security and income which constrained the poor in obtaining access to credit rather than on devising innovative means to offset the higher costs inherent in delivering Banking services to the poor. Given unrealistically low-fixed interest rates on priority rural credit, the high costs associated with lending small amounts to large numbers of scattered borrowers were the primary causes of market failure. The Committee recognized that individual, scattered or adhoc approach to lending, which did not take into account an area plan and the demand for credit, could result in increasing indebtedness of the poor instead of credit, serving as an instrument for poverty alleviation. Yet, the IRD emphasised on targets, expenditures and supply of credit for individual households. It did not foster an integrated or demand-led approach to lending.

Credit schemes operated by the Banking system for poverty-alleviation have proliferated in recent years. In addition to Integrated Rural Development Programme, which is the largest, other Banks also provide credit on favourable terms and subsidies besides the other programmes of the government 20 Point Programme for development. The most recent institutional response to the problem of how to provide Service Area Scheme (SAS) has become effective for all Banks since January 1, 1989. This approach is a quantum-step beyond the earlier 'Lead Bank Scheme' (LBS) which attempted to co-ordinate Bank activity within a district, since it assigns 20 villages exclusively to each branch for lending purpose. Banks are expected to survey forward and backward linkages available in their service-area and then offer finance for viable investment. This continues to be the permanent pre-occupation with supply-driven credit and macro-level earning, where district and Blocks have apparently failed in the past to ensure adequate linkages, Banks have now been assigned this task.

INSTITUTIONAL SOURCES OF CREDIT

The rural credit system in India consists of two types viz., institutional and non-institutional credit. The non-institutional credit consists mainly, professional and agricultural money-lenders, landlords, traders, commission agents and relatives and friends. According to all India Rural Credit Survey Committee's observation, during 1951-52, the share of non-institutional credit accounted for about 94 per cent; the share of institutional credit, the Co-operatives and Government accounted for 6.4 per cent; Commercial Banks for just 0.9 per cent. This can be seen in Table—3.1.

Table—3.1

Institutional and Non-Institutional Credit

Sl. No	*Credit Agency*	*Proportion in the borrowings (per cent)*
1.	Government	3.3
2.	Co-operatives	3.1
3.	Commercial Banks	0.9
4.	Relatives	14.2
5.	Agriculturist money-lenders	24.9
6.	Professional money-lenders	44.8
7.	Others	8.8
	Total	100.00

Source: RBI; CRAFICARD; Bombay, 1981, p. 400.

However, the share of non-institutional credit in total borrowings of farmers has recorded a decline from more than

94 in 1951-52 to 85 per cent in 1961-62, and 75 per cent in 1971-72[2] and to about 65 per cent at present. In the estimation of the National Credit Council the various institutional credit agencies like Co-operatives, Commercial and Regional Rural Banks met only 38 per cent of the estimated credit requirements of agriculture in 1967-68. There have been only marginal improvement in this position.[3] After the introduction of social control over Banks, the Banks are taking special care for agriculture development by improving their share of credit for agriculture.

The need for institutional credit arises because of the weakness of inadequacy of private agencies to supply credit to farmers. Private credit is defective because:

(i) it is based on profit motive and it is always positive;

(ii) it is expensive;

(iii) it does not flow into most desirable channels and most needy persons;

(iv) it is not available for making agricultural improvements on long-terms basis; and

(v) it is not properly integrated with the agriculturists' other needs.

Institutional credit is never explanative and its basic motive is always to help the farmers to raise his productivity and maximise his income. The rate of interest is very low. Institutions also make a clear distinction between short-term credit and long-term credit requirements and give loans accordingly. Institutional credit is fully integrated with others needs of Agriculturalists. The farmers require not only credit but also training in agricultural operations like the use of seeds, fertilizers and pesticides etc. besides assistance in raising crops and in general, help for maximising their income. In all developed countries, credit services and extension services go hand in hand. This work can be done best by institutions like Co-operative Societies and Commercial Banks and but by rapacious money-lenders and commission agents.

CO-OPERATIVE BANKS IN INDIA

Introduction

In the Banking system of India, primarily Commercial Banks and Co-operative Banks play a greater role. They occupy a significant place in the economy of India. Commercial Banks have concentrated their attention on industries and business, whereas Co-operative Banks extend their assistance to agriculture.

The genesis of Co-operative Banks can be attributed to the co-operative principles. The association joined together for mutual benefit, can be called as a co-operative institution. Despite the varying amount of capital contribution by different individuals, all the members enjoy equal voting rights. Thus all the members enjoy benefits equally on the basis of co-operative principles.

Co-operative Movement started in India in the early days of the 20th Century i.e., 1904. In those days, agriculturists completely depended on pawn-brokers, and money-lenders, for their extra-income needs. Pawn-brokers and money-lenders used to cheat the agriculturists. To overcome and to free them from these money squeezers (money-lenders and pawn-brokers) and to get rid the agriculturists from the clutches of the money-lenders, Co-operative Movement was started to help the innocent rural people.

The First Co-operative Act came into existence in the year 1904. Soon after the introduction of the Co-operative Act, in various places of the country, Co-operative Societies were started. But these Societies failed to serve the need and requirements of the agriculturalists. Hence, for the establishment of Central Co-operative Banks, another Co-operative Act came into existence in the year 1912.

MC GLAN COMMITTEE

To know the changes that have taken place in the Co-operative sector, in the year 1914, the Government formed a Committee under the Chairmanship of Mr. MC Glan. The Committee, in their findings, felt the needs of a Co-operative

Federation at the State level, to bring unity amongst the activities of various Co-operative Banks. The Government, after careful consideration of the findings of MC Glan Committee, started Co-operative Federation in various States. With this, the activities of Co-operative Banks extended even to non-agricultural sector.

THREE-TIER SYSTEM

Due to the establishment of Co-operative Banks at different levels, a three-tier system came to existence in India. At village level, primary co-operative societies; at District level Central Co-operative Banks; and at State level, State Co-operative Banks are functioning at present. In the year 1982, at the National level, a National Co-operative Bank was established. The functioning of various Co-operative Banks can be understood with the help of the diagram (Chart—3.1).

TYPES OF CO-OPERATIVE BANKS

The financial requirement of agriculturists is of three types. (1) Short-term, (2) Medium-term and (3) Long-term. The short-term credit period is between 12-18 months. The financial assistance helps the farmers in purchasing seeds, in paying labour charges and in the purchase of fertilizers. Medium-term loans are of 2 years time period; and long-term loans are 6-15 years period.

Taking the needs of the farmers into consideration, the three-tier system has been implemented in India. (1) Primary Co-operative Banks, (?) District Central Co-operative Banks, (3) State Co-operative Banks.

PRIMARY CO-OPERATIVE BANKS

Keeping in view the needs of village-based farmers, Primary Co-operative Banks were started. These Banks keep direct relationship with farmers and serve their short-term credit needs.

A minimum number of 10 people can start a Co-operative Bank. Every member has to pay his share of capital to the Society towards his membership. Any person, living in the geographical limits of a particular village, can join as a member of the village Co-operative Banks.

Chart—3.1
Co-operative Credit System

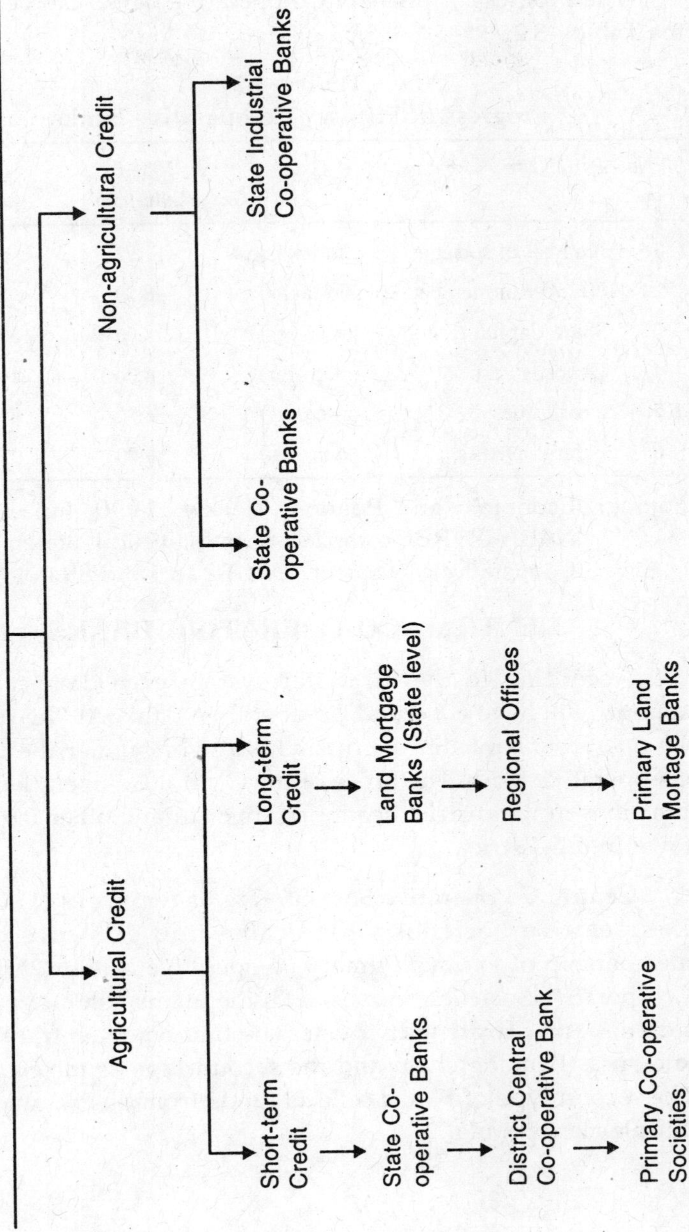

The progress of primary Co-operative Banks can be seen in the Table—3.2.

Table—3.2
Progress of Primary Co-operative Banks

Sl. No.	*Particulars*		*1951-52 (July-June)*	*1988-89 (July-June)*
1.	Number of societies	(in lakhs)	1.92	2.08
2.	Number of members	(in lakhs)	48.00	866.69
3.	Share Capital reserves	(in crores)	18.00	1957.00
4.	Deposits	(in crores)	4.00	1464.00
5.	Credit dues	(in crores)	34.00	4554.00
6.	Expired credits	(in crores)	9.00	2238.00

Source: Economic and Political Weekly, 1990 June, p. 28. NABARD/RBI compiled from Statistical Statements to Cooperative Movement 1951-52 to 1988-89.

CENTRAL CO-OPERATIVE BANKS

According to the three-tier system each district in the country will have a Central Co-operative Bank. All the primary Co-operative Banks in the district will work under the Central Co-operative Bank. The office of the Central Co-operative Bank, functions in the district headquarters or in any other important town in the district.

Central Co-operative Societies are or two types (1) Central Co-operative Societies which came into existence by the membership of various primary co-operative banks. (2) Central Co-operative Societies, formed with the membership of primary societies and private individuals. The first type, Central Bank is known as Banking chain and the second type as mixed Banks. The second type of Banks collects funds from businessmen and middle-class people.

MEMBERSHIP

Besides Primary Co-operative Banks, marketing societies, consumers stores, agricultural associations, town-Co-operative Societies also can seek membership in the Central Co-operative Banks.

ADMINISTRATION

The administrative responsibilities of the Central Banks lie in the hands of elected Board of Directors. The number of Directors in the Bank Board is between 12 and 15.

Table—3.3
Progress of Central Co-operative Banks

Sl. No.	*Particulars*		*1951-52 (July-June)*	*1989-90 (July-June)*
1.	Number of Banks		509	349
2.	Capital Reserves	(in Crores)	10	1,900
3.	Deposits	(in Crores)	38	5,766
4.	Credit dues	(in Crores)	36	9,707
5.	Expired credit	(in Crores)	5	2,567

Source: Economic Times, November 4, 1990, p. 13.

The above table reveals that the Central Co-operative Banks, progressed rapidly in proportion to the growth of the primary Co-operative Banks. Central Banks provide financial assistance to the primary Co-operative Banks; thus helps the rural farmers a lot. Not only this, the Bank also collects excessive funds from the primary Co-operative Banks and helps other membership-Banks in meeting their requirements.

STATE CO-OPERATIVE BANKS

Like the primary Co-operative Banks in villages, Central Co-operative Banks in Districts, the State Co-operative Banks functioning at the State level, the District Co-operative Banks and primary Co-operative Banks may seek the membership in the State Co-operative Banks. Even individuals are allowed to take membership.

FINANCIAL RESOURCES

The financial resources of the Central Co-operative Banks are mainly the share capital, reserve fund, various deposits, cash credits from Commercial Banks overdrafts and the surplus funds of the affiliated Central Co-operative Banks. Among these, Reserve Bank funds stand higher in amount.

With the help of Table—3.4, one can say that there is remarkable progress in the functioning of the State Co-operative Banks. In the year 1951, it started its functions with only Rs. 4 crores as capital and, at present, it amounts to Rs. 544 crores, capital and reserves.

Table—3.4
Progress of State Co-operative Banks

Sl. No.	Particulars		1951-52	1983-85
1.	Number of Banks		16	28
2.	Capital reserve	(in crores)	4	544
3.	Deposits	(in crores)	21	3,556
4.	Credit dues	(in crores)	20	4,916
	Expired credit	(in crores)	3	478

Source: Reserve Bank of India Report on Trend and Progress of Banking in India, 1989-90, p. 138.

LAND DEVELOPMENT BANKS

Land Development Banks are of two types:

1. Central Land Development Bank.
2. Primary Land Development Bank.

Every State will have a Central Co-operative Bank. Primary Co-operative Banks at the taluk or district level work with the affiliation of the Central Co-operative Bank.

SINGLE-WINDOW SCHEME

In Andhra Pradesh, to integrate the various activities of the Primary Co-operative Banks and District Central Co-operative

Banks with the State Co-operative Banks and to make available both the short-term, medium-term and long-term at the same bank, the Government has brought all the Co-operative Banks under the jurisdiction of State Co-operative Bank, this integration has benefited the farmers a lot.

COMMERCIAL BANKS—RURAL DEVELOPMENT

Emergence of Commercial Banks

Apart from the weakness observed in the working of Co-operative Societies, the major reasons for changing the policy of entrusting to the Co-operatives the 'sole' responsibility of purveying credit are as follows : (1) the substantial spurt in the demand for rural credit as a result of the breakthrough in the evolution of the high-yielding varieties and consequent demand for costly inputs such as chemical fertilisers, and pesticides etc., (2) the development of irrigation facilities by way of dependable sources of water for ensuring the success of high-yielding varieties programme. The National Commission on Agriculture emphasised the urgent need for strengthening of the credit structure. Against this background, it was increasingly felt that Commercial Banks could supplement the efforts of the Co-operative Societies to meet the credit needs of agriculture and non-agriculture. Introduction of the scheme of social control over Commercial Banks in 1968 and liberalising of the National Commercial Banks credit towards agriculture and non-agriculture, on 'priority' basis. Bank lending targets were laid for the Banking system in respect of the development of funds for agriculture and other priority sectors. Banks were encouraged to lend their support to agriculture.

Operations of Commercial Banks

Till recently, Indian Banks, by and large operated in urban centres and provided credit to trade and industry, commerce etc. But they neglected agriculture and rural development in particular and rural economy in general. It is only after nationalisation, the attention of these Banks was focused on rural areas. The real beginning for setting up of Rural Banks was suggested by Banking Commission in its Report in 1972.[4] It was the opinion of Commission that in rural areas Commercial Banks failed to expand Bank branches and to extend credit to farmfamilies. Further, the Committee suggested setting up of a new class of rural Banks in areas where co-operatives were weak. The Committee in its Report also stated that these Banks should meet the full credit needs of small farmers, handloom labourers, artisans and craftsmen etc.

Though NABARD is solely made responsible for financing agricultural and rural development, at present, various agencies such as RRBs, Commercial Banks and Co-operative Banks etc., are working in the field of rural finance.

The Banking system of the country has witnessed tremendous changes since their nationalisation. Commercial Banks were originally established in India by big industrialist and business houses. They concentrated on urban areas and catered only to big industrialists; it was they who could obtain necessary financial help from them. These Banks were least interested in financing agricultural and rural development. This lacuna in functioning of Scheduled Commercial Banks was noted by the Government with serious concern, especially after the ushering in of Green Revolution in the country. To meet the credit requirements of the new strategy, fourteen (14) Commercial Banks were nationalised in 1969, again in the second phase of nationalisation (1980), six other Commercial Banks were nationalised. All theses Banks have shown fortunately an impressive aggregate-record-of-performance in almost all the spheres of their activities.

Share of Commercial Banks' Finance in Rural Development

The share of the Commercial Banks' finance in total rural finance has considerably increased in recent years. For example, before the nationalisation, the share of the Commercial Banks in the total borrowings of the farm sector was hardly 5.3 per cent in 1967-68. Subsequently it increased to 34.4 per cent in 1980-81.[5]

Pattern of Advances

Commercial Banks have made excellent progress in providing direct finance to agriculture. The direct finance increased from 32 per cent in 1967-68 to about 75.2 per cent in 1979-80, indirect finance decreased from 68 per cent to 24.8 per cent of the total advance to agriculture during the same period.[6]

Apart from financing the farmers, both directly and indirectly for agricultural and rural development, the Commercial Banks are also helping and promoting financing institutions, financial development schemes, Agricultural Development Departments and are actively involved in the rural development programmes. For instance, all most all nationalised Banks have embraced village-adoption scheme. The important feature of the Scheme is all round development of the village economy. The Banks are actively involved in the preparation of village level credit-plans as well as in the implementation of the same. So far, they have adopted more than 270 schemes and have provided assistance to the tune of Rs. 449 crores.

From the above account, it is clear that the Commercial Banks have taken up on themselves a big task of agricultural development, subsidy occupations and rural area development schemes. Thus, credit for development of agriculture and various rural area development programmes has been made through various schemes and programmes tailored to suit the emerging conditions of socio-economic groups in the villages. These Banks have also set up RRBs for assisting the rural and down-trodden families.

Performance of Commercial Banks

The branch network of Commercial Banks in rural and semi-urban areas have expanded from 28,786 in June 1989 to 30, 153 in June 1990, registering an increase of 11.69 per cent over the previous year. The outstanding direct agricultural advances by all the scheduled Commercial Banks rose considerably, in absolute terms, from Rs. 7,988 crores as on 30th June 1989 to Rs. 12,891 crores as on June 1990.

Based on the positions as on 30th June 1989, only 6,577 of the 25,165 reporting branches of Commercial Banks enjoyed unrestricted eligibility for re-finance from the National Bank by virtue of maintaining a recovery level of 75 per cent or more of the demand. Of the remaining 18,608 branches, only 2,894 had moderate-eligibility for re-finance and 15,714 branches had lowest eligibility.

GENESIS OF REGIONAL RURAL BANKS

Finance is an essential and important input for breaking the vicious circle of poverty. The Co-operatives, started in 1904 in our country, were well entrenched and were the only financing agency in rural areas till the acceptance of the principle of multiagency approach brought the Commercial Banks in rural credit scenario. Though they failed in some areas, the Government had been thinking on steps to organise them on strong and viable lines. Until the introduction of social control in the sphere of Banking in 1968, it was official policy to develop the Co-operative system as the sole agency for meeting agricultural-credit requirements. However, Co-operatives had been suffering from certain handicaps like (i) lack of managerial competence, (ii) lack of aggressiveness in resource mobilisation. The Green Revolution and modernisation of agriculture, witnessed from late sixties, necessitated higher credit requirements which Co-operatives alone failed to meet. This resulted credit culminating in social control of Banks in 1968; the nationalisation of fourteen major Commercial Banks. Since then, Commercial Banks as a matter of policy have been involved in the sphere of agricultural finance. But, the experience of Commercial Bank branches, in rural areas in financing agriculture, has revealed that they failed to cater to the credit requirements of specific groups like small and marginal farmers and agricultural labourers etc. It was observed that rural branches of Commercial Banks suffered from two basic setbacks:

(i) fairly high cost structure resulting from high salaries of staff; and

(ii) the absence of staff with proper approach, orientation and training to deal with rural clientele and problems of agricultural finance.

Emergency was imposed in the country and "a new economic programme" (20 Point Programme) was declared. This programme aimed at, inter alia "devising alternative agencies to provide institutional credit to landless labourers, rural artisans and small and marginal farmers and agricultural labourers etc.".

Responding this situation the Government of India set up a Committee, under the Chairmanship of Sri. M. Narasimham[7], was appointed on July 1, 1975, to examine in-depth the setting up of new rural Banks and subsidiaries of Public Sector Banks to cater to the credit-needs of the rural poor. This group opined that Co-operatives and Commercial Banks would not be able to fill the regional and functional gap in the rural credit system within a reasonable period of time. The group felt that in a country of the size and regional diversity as ours, no single pattern belt of Commercial Banks or Co-operative can be expected to meet all the emerging requirements in all areas. A degree of adoption and improvisation was called for and the range of institutional alternatives widened. In this context they came to the conclusion that a new type of institution was necessary. It, therefore, recommended the setting up of the State-sponsored, region-based and rural-oriented Commercial Banks called Regional Rural Banks. The group recommended the establishment of some 4 or 5 Regional Rural Banks on experimental basis largely with a view to meet the credit gaps in areas opened up or to be opened for large agricultural development projects. The RRB's, according to the group, are expected to combine in themselves the local touch and low cost of operations of the Co-operatives and efficient managerial skills and commercial principles of rural branches of Commercial Banks while avoiding the weaknesses of both.

Accepting the recommendations of the working group, the Government of India promulgated the Regional Rural Bank Ordinance on September 26, 1975, and the first Regional Rural Banks in different States like, Haryana-1; Rajasthan-1; Bihar-1 West Bengal-1; and Uttar Pradesh-1. The ordinance was replaced by the Regional Rural Banks Act made by Parliament on

9th February 1976.[8] RRBs thus came to from the third component of multi-agency credit system for agriculture and Rural Development.

Salient Features of Regional Rural Banks

Regional Rural Banks are poorman's banks, which identify the problems of neglected sectors of the community and endeavours to mitigate their difficulties by increasing their income in a phased manner by extending the financial assistance to further their professions.

They lend either directly of through the Primary Agricultural Credit Societies, preferably through Farmers' Service Societies. The rules and regulations are simple and can be understood very easily by the ruralfolk, as far as possible, the Banks will transact the business in the local language.

Structure and Organisational Set up of RRBs

This Act was passed to provide for the incorporation, regulation and widening up of Regional Rural Banks with a view to developing the rural economy by providing for the purpose of development of agriculture, trade, commerce, industry and other productive activities in the rural areas; credit and other facilities particularly to the small and marginal farmers and agricultural and non-agricultural labourers, artisans and small entrepreneurs.[9] The Regional Rural Banks Act extended to the whole of India and came into force with retrospective effect i.e., 26-9-1975. The following provisions were found in this Act : The Central Government, on request of a sponsor Bank, may establish in a State or Union Territory one or more Regional Rural Banks through notification in the official Gazette. Such RRBs shall have the name and operational area as decided by the Central Government and shall have its head office at such place within the notified area as notified by Central Government in consultation with sponsor Bank and RBI. Except, the Chairman, RRBs can appoint all the staff i.e., Branch Managers, Field Officers, Clerks, Cashiers etc. Those within an operational jurisdiction of the respective RRB and with rural knowledge and orientation are to be selected on the staff with active secretarial assistance from the sponsoring bank. This would mean that the staff is familiar with the local language and environment. The Regional Rural Banks have been evolved as low-cost and rural-based institutions and, therefore, eminently suited to implement bankable schemes in the rural areas.[10]

The remuneration of officers and other employees of Regional Rural Banks shall be determined by the Central Government having due regard to the salary structure of the employees of the state Government and local authorities of comparable level in the notified area. Thus they have an altogether different salary structure from the one prevailing in Commercial Banks.

Incorporation and Capital of Regional Rural Banks

Every Regional Rural Bank in a body corporate with perpetual succession and a common seal with power, subject to the provisions of this Act, requires to hold and dispose of property and to contract and may sue and be sued in its name.

The authorised capital of each Regional Rural Bank shall be one crore of rupees, divided into one lakh of fully paid up shares of one hundred rupees each. The Central Government may increase or deduce the authorised capital in consultation with the Reserve Bank of India and the sponsor Bank but the capital cannot be reduced below twenty five lakhs of rupees and the share of value below Rs. 100 each.

The issued capital of each RRB shall be twenty five lakh of rupees of which fifty per cent shall be subscribed by the Central Government, fifteen per cent by the concerned State Government and thirty five percent by the sponsor Bank. The issued capital can be increased from time to time by the Board of the Bank in consultation with the Reserve Bank, the sponsor Bank and the concerned State Government and with the prior approval of the Central Government such addition shall be subscribed by the shareholders in the same proportion as stated above.

Management

According to this Act, the general superintendence, direction and management of the affairs and business of a RRB is vested in a Board of Directors. The Board is required to enact any business principles having due regard to public interest. A Regional Rural Bank, in discharging its functions, will be guided by the directions of the Central Government in regard to policy matters involving public interest.

The Board of Directors consists of a Chairman, not more than three Directors to be nominated by Central Government, not more than three Directors to be nominated by the sponsor Bank. The Central Government may increase the number of members of the Board, subject, however, to the maximum of 15 in the aggregate. A Director other than the Chairman shall hold office for two years or any other specified period when the nomination is made. He is also eligible for renomination. The Chairman is appointed by Central Government for a specified period not exceeding five years. He shall devote wholetime for the affairs of the Bank. He shall be re-eligible for re-appointment. The Chairman shall have subject to the superintendence, control and direction of the Board, the management of the whole of the affairs of the Regional Rural Bank.

Business of a Regional Rural Bank

Regional Rural Bank has to carry on and transact the business, the business of Banking as defined in Clause (b) of Section 5 of the Banking Regulation Act, 1949, and may engage in one or more forms of business specified in Sub Section (1) of Section 6 of that Act. The RRB is to undertake

(a) the granting of loans and advances, particularly to small and marginal farmers and agricultural labourers whether individually or in group;

(b) the granting of loans and advances to Co-operative Societies including agricultural marketing societies, agricultural processing societies, co-operative farming societies, primary agricultural credit societies of faramers service societies for agricultural purpose of

agricultural operations or for other purposes connected therewith;

(c) the granting of loans and advances, particularly to artisans, small entrepreneurs and persons of small means engaged in trade, commerce or industry of other productive activities within the notified area in relation to the Regional Rural Banks.

OPERATIONAL EFFICIENCY OF REGIONAL RURAL BANK

Progress of RRBs

Every Regional Rural Bank (RRB) is sponsored by a Scheduled Commercial Bank, usually Public Sector Bank. A few non-public sector Banks have also sponsored Regional Rural Banks. Following the decision taken by the Reserve Bank of India in consultation with the Government of India, State Co-operative Banks are also allowed to sponsor RRBs. The sponsoring Bank of the districts fall within the operational jurisdiction of the Regional Rural Bank sponsored by it. The sponsor Bank has certain duties towards the Regional Rural Bank by it. It shall be the study of the sponsor Bank to aid and assist the RRB sponsored by it, by subscribing to the share capital of such Regional Rural Bank, recruitment and training of personnel during the first five years of the functioning of the RRB and providing such managerial and financial assistance as may be mutually agreed upon between the sponsor Bank and the RRB. The sponsor Bank provides refinance facility, nominates Directors to the Board from time to time and recommends the name of a person who has to be appointed as the Chairman of the RRB.

Generally, the operational area of each RRB is confined to a compact area of one to three revenue districts with homogenity in agro-climatic conditions and rural clientele. The economic backwardness of some of the Districts have also been weighed favourably for the solution of locating the rural Banks. The RRBs were to open their branches in the un-Banked and under-Banked centers where the Primary Agricultural Credit Societies (PACS) and Commercial Banks are weak and unable to cater to the needs of weaker sections.

As referred earlier, the Regional Rural Banks (RRBs) were inaugurated on 2nd October, 1975. The first five RRBs were established on 2-10-1975. The first Regional Rural Bank established was the Prathama Bank in Muradabad district of Uttar Pradesh, sponsored by Syndicate Bank. Other remaining Banks were also started on the same day. One more RRB was started on 26th December 1975 in Bihar by Punjab National Bank. Since the inception of these banks, the number of RRBs established in the country, had gone upto 196 at the end of December 1989.

Initially, in the last quarter of 1975, there were only 6 RRBs but their number increased to 40 by the end of 1976. Thus, in 1976 alone 34 RRBs were set up but this tempo was not kept up in the next three years 1977-79 as there were some reservations and fresh thinking about the speed with which new RRBs should be opened up. But in view of the strong recommendations of the Dantwala Committee, there was a sharp increase in the number of RRBs in the following years. Thus, during the year 1980, 25 RRBs were established covering with additional 33 districts covering the geographical area of 144 districts with total 85 RRBs. Again in 1983, another 65 RRBs were opened making the total 150 RRBs, covering the geographical area of 265 districts. In the subsequent years, however, there was a fall in the growth of the RRBs. By the end of 1989 March, there were 196 RRBs covering 369 districts in the country.

The number of branches initially i.e., in 1975 were only 17. By December 1976, 40 RRBs operated through 489 branches with growth of 472 branches, with an average number of branches per RRB 12. The position improved substantially and by the end of March 1989 there were 14,029 branches, with the growth of 159 branches, an average number of branches per RRB 72. A large number of branches were opened in the year 1984 (2,450); and in the year 1985 (2,361), though there was a rapid fall in the year 1989 (159). The average number of branches per RRB also increased from mere 3 in 1975, to 72 in 1989. Progress achieved by RRBs in expanding their network, their coverage of districts etc., is shown in Table—3.5.

Table—3.5
Progress of Regional Rural Banks

Sl. No.	*At the end of December*	*No. of RRBs*	*No. of branches*	*District covered*	*Growth in RRBs*	*Growth in Branches*	*Average No. of branches per RRB*
1.	1975	6	17	12	–	–	3
2.	1976	40	489	84	34	472	12
3.	1977	48	1187	99	8	698	25
4.	1978	51	1753	102	3	566	34
5.	1979	60	2420	111	9	667	40
6.	1980	85	3279	144	25	859	39
7.	1981	107	4795	182	22	1516	43
8.	1982	124	6191	214	17	1896	50
9.	1983	150	7795	265	26	1604	52
10.	1984	173	10245	307	23	2450	59
11.	1985	188	12606	333	15	2361	67
12.	1986	194	12838	351	6	232	66
13.	1987	196	13553	363	2	232	69
14.	1988	196	13920	369	–	715	71
15.	1989 March	196*	14079	369	–	159	72

*Note** : Consequent upon bifurcation of existing districts.

Source: Statistics on Regional Rural Banks, Regional Rural Banks Division, NABARD, Bombay, 1989.

Table—3.6 shows the state-wise and year-wise growth in Regional Rural Banks and the districts covered by them. As at the end of March 1989, Uttar Pradesh and largest number of RRBs (40) followed by Madhya Pradesh (24), Bihar (22), Andhra Pradesh (16), Rajasthan (14) and Karnataka (13), Maharashtra (10), Gujarat (9), West Bengal (9), Orissa (9), Punjab (5), Haryana (4), Jammu & Kashmir and Tamil Nadu each having only 3 RRBs, Kerala and Himachal Pradesh each having 2, Arunachal Pradesh, Manipur, Meghalaya, Mizoram, Nagaland, Tripura each State having only one RRB.

The Table—3.7 shows the region-wise and State-wise bank loans issued under special programmes at the end of March 1991. Under Integrated Rural Development Programme (IRDP), the total number of accounts, all India-wise to 8,51,472. Among these accounts, the highest number of accounts, 3,47,622 is in the Central Region having highest number of accounts 3,47,622 which is followed by eastern region 2,28,486. Among State-wise, the highest number of IRDP accounts is highest in Uttar Pradesh 2,26,874, which is followed by Bihar 1,28,191 accounts.

In respect of Integrated Rural Development amount sanctioned total, all India-wise, Rs. 26316.15 lakhs. Among these, Central region Rs. 10775.43 lakh distributed for rural development, followed by eastern region Rs. 6515.05 lakhs distributed for rural deveiopment. In respect of States, distributed for IRDP amount, highest distribution is Rs. 7143.43 lakh Uttar Pradesh which is followed by Bihar Rs. 4127.37 lakhs. The least amount is given for IRDP was Meghalaya Rs. 0.71 lakhs.

Under differential rate of interest-rate number of accounts all India-wise are having 19,381 accounts. Among these region-wise distribution of accounts under differential rate of interest scheme, northern region has highest number of accounts 4,954, which is followed by central region 4,779 accounts; Jammu & Kashmir having lowest number of accounts 3.

Table—3.6

Statement showing the State-wise, Year-wise Growth in RRBs and the number of districts covered

Sl. No.	State/ Union Territories	1975	1976	1977	1978	1979	1980	1981	1982	1983	1984	1985	1986	1987	1988	1989	1990	No. of RRBs Total
I.	**Northern Region**																	
1.	Haryana	1 (4)	1 (3)	-	-	-	-	-	-	-	1 (2)	1 (2)	-	-	-	-	-	4 (11)
2.	Himachal Pradesh	-	1 (3)	-	-	-	-	-	-	-	-	1 (1)	-	-	-	-	-	2 (4)
3.	Jammu & Kashmir	-	1 (4)	-	-	1 (4)	-	1 (2)	-	-	-	-	-	-	-	-	-	3 (10)
4.	Punjab	-	-	-	-	-	-	-	-	3 (6)	-	-	2 (4)	-	-	-	-	5 (10)
5.	Rajasthan	1 (2)	2 (5)	-	-	1 (1)	-	2 (5)	1 (2)	2 (4)	4 (7)	1 (1)	-	-	-	-	-	14 (27)
																		28 (62)
II.	**North-Eastern Region**																	
6.	Arunachal Pradesh	-	-	-	-	-	-	-	-	1 (4)	-	-	-	-	-	-	-	1 (4)
7.	Assam	-	1 (9)	-	-	-	1 (5)	1 (2)	2 (4)	-	-	-	-	-	-	-	-	5 (20)
8.	Manipur	-	-	-	-	-	-	1 (8)	-	-	-	-	-	-	-	-	-	1 (8)
9.	Meghalaya	-	-	-	-	-	-	1 (3)	-	-	-	-	-	-	-	-	-	1 (3)
10.	Mizoram	-	-	-	-	-	-	-	-	1 (3)	-	-	-	-	-	-	-	1 (3)
11.	Nagaland	-	-	-	-	-	-	-	-	1 (7)	-	-	-	-	-	-	-	1 (7)
12.	Triprua	-	1 (3)	-	-	-	-	-	-	-	-	-	-	-	-	-		1 (3)
																		11 (45)

(Tables contd. ...)

Sl. No.	State/ Union Territories	1975	1976	1977	1978	1979	1980	1981	1982	1983	1984	1985	1986	1987	1988	1989	1990	No. of RRBs Total
III.	**Eastern Region**																	
13.	Bihar	1 (2)	3 (10)	3 (9)	-	3 (3)	4 (6)	3 (3)	-	-	3 (3)	2 (2)	-	-	-	-	-	22 (38)
14.	Orissa	-	4 (5)	-	-	-	3 (5)	2 (2)	-	-	-	-	-	-	-	-	-	9 (13)
15.	West Bengal	1 (3)	2 (4)	1 (3)	-	-	3 (5)	-	1 (2)	-	1 (1)	-	-	-	-	-	-	9 (18)
																		40 (69)
IV.	**Central Region**																	
16.	Madhya Pradesh	-	3 (6)	1 (2)	-	3 (3)	2 (4)	3 (6)	3 (6)	4 (7)	3 (6)	1 (2)	1 (2)	-	-	-	-	24 (44)
17.	Uttar Pradesh	2 (4)	6 (8)	2 (4)	-	-	12 (14)	5 (5)	2 (4)	6 (8)	1 (1)	3 (6)	-	1 (2)	-	-	-	40 (56)
																		64 (100)
V.	**Western Region**																	
18.	Gujarat	-	-	-	2 (3)	-	-	1 (2)	1 (2)	1 (2)	4 (8)	-	-	-	-	-	-	9 (17)
19.	Maharashtra	-	1 (5)	-	-	-	-	-	1 (2)	3 (5)	2 (2)	2 (2)	1 (1)	-	-	-	-	10 (17)
																		19 (34)
VI.	**Southern Region**																	
20.	Andhra Pradesh	-	3 (8)	-	-	1 (1)	-	1 (1)	5 (6)	2 (2)	-	2 (2)	1 (1)	1 (2)	-	-	-	16 (23)
21.	Karnataka	-	3 (6)	-	1 (2)	-	-	1 (1)	1 (3)	2 (2)	4 (5)	1 (1)	-	-	-	-	-	13 (20)
22.	Kerala	-	2 (6)	-	-	-	-	-	-	-	-	-	-	-	-	-	-	2 (6)
23.	Tamil Nadu	-	-	1 (5)	-	-	-	-	-	-	-	1 (1)	1 (1)	-	-	-	-	3 (7)
	Total All India	6 (15)	34 (86)	8 (23)	3 (5)	9 (12)	25 (39)	22 (40)	17 (31)	26 (50)	23 (35)	15 (20)	6 (9)	2 (9)	-	-	-	196 (369)

Source : Statistics on Regional Rural Banks, NABARD, Region, Bombay, 1989,

Note : Figures in brackets indicate number of districts covered.

Table—3.7
Region/State-wise Bank Loans issued under Special Programmes from 1988 April to March 1991

(Rs. in lakhs)

Sl. No.	Name of the State/ Region	IRDP		DRI		Others		Total	
		No. of accounts	Amount	No. of accounts	Amount	No. of accounts	Amount	No. of accounts	Amount
	1	2	3	4	5	6	7	8	9
1.	Haryana	21831	818.88	1560	76.20	229	6.81	23620	901.89
2.	Himachal Pradesh	4875	174.91	1663	26.21	1162	8.14	7700	209.66
3.	Jammu & Kashmir	8177	321.35	3	0.07	41	2.55	8221	323.97
4.	Punjab	9502	301.28	548	23.25	1869	97.86	11919	422.39
5.	Rajasthan	42913	1092.45	1180	37.16	2421	111.52	46514	1241.13
	Northern Region	**87298**	**2708.87**	**4954**	**162.89**	**5722**	**226.88**	**97974**	**3099.04**
6.	Arunachal Pradesh	271	7.44	17	0.36	-	-	288	7.80
7.	Assam	18174	633.03	957	25.92	911	19.15	20042	678.10
8.	Manipur	675	26.21	-	-	-	-	673	26.21
9.	Meghalaya	34	0.71	220	1.85	-	-	254	2.56
10.	Mizoram	805	21.13	207	5.88	-	-	1012	27.01
11.	Nagaland	62	2.68	-	-	-	-	62	2.68
12.	Tripura	30690	581.27	-	-	-	-	30690	581.27
	North-Eastern Region	**50711**	**1272.47**	**1401**	**34.01**	**911**	**19.15**	**53021**	**1325.63**

(Table contd. ...)

	1	2	3	4	5	6	7	8	9
13.	Bihar	128191	4197.37	966	31.47	1089	64.02	130253	4222.86
14.	Orissa	49223	1141.26	3138	67.95	17822	311.94	70183	1521.15
15.	West Bengal	51065	1246.42	179	3.12	17835	246.09	69079	1495.63
	Eastern Region	**228479**	**6515.05**	**4283**	**102.54**	**36746**	**622.05**	**269515**	**7239.64**
16.	Maharashtra	24085	745.79	16	0.34	3237	154.38	27338	900.51
	Western Region	**42117**	**1366.32**	**119**	**5.48**	**11409**	**460.33**	**53645**	**1832.15**
17.	Andhra Pradesh	34621	1408.57	546	4.60	29485	1014.28	64652	2427.45
18.	Madhya Pradesh	120748	3630.00	719	11.78	10439	453.63	131906	4095.41
19.	Uttar Pradesh	226874	7143.43	4060	143.38	12546	509.79	243480	7796.60
	Central Region	**347622**	**10773.43**	**4779**	**155.16**	**22985**	**963.42**	**375386**	**11892.01**
20.	Gujarat	18032	620.53	103	5.14	8172	305.97	26307	931.64
21.	Karnataka	34403	1236.84	1390	35.68	6312	335.91	42105	1608.69
22.	Kerala	10083	327.63	1811	8.78	333	16.80	12227	353.21
23.	Tamil Nadu	16133	706.97	98	1.02	3566	140.36	19797	848.35
	Southern Region	**78651**	**2891.97**	**3402**	**50.62**	**18383**	**799.04**	**100436**	**3741.89**
	All India	851472	26316.15	19381	510.56	117469	3799.26	988322	30625.97

Source: Statistics on Regional Rural Banks, NABARD, Bombay, RRB Divison, 1991, pp. 52-59.

In respect of amount under DRI, all India-wide in 1991 having Rs. 510.70 lakhs. In region-wise, the highest amount under DRI was Rs. 162.89 lakhs in northern region, followed by central region Rs. 155.16 lakhs. In this respect, States having amount of rupees under DRI, the State having Rs. 143.38 lakhs amount in Uttar Pradesh, followed by Haryana Rs. 76.20 lakhs of amount under DRI scheme. The least amount under DRI is Rs. 0.07 lakhs.

In the year 1991, Bank loans issued under special scheme like IRDP, DRI and others come to total number of accounts, all India-wide, is 9,88,322 accounts. Among all these different schemes accounts 3,75,386, the highest in central region, followed by southern region 1,38,781 accounts. In respect of States, the highest number of accounts having in different schemes is 2,43,480 Uttar Pradesh, followed by Bihar 1,30,253 accounts.

In respect of money issued under different schemes in the year 1989 was Rs. 30625.97 lakhs. Among these amount, region-wise, it stands the highest amount. Issued central regions with an amount of Rs. 11892.01 lakhs which is followed by southern region Rs. 3741.89 lakhs, and the least amount issued region is north eastern region Rs. 1325.63 lakhs. The individual states issued under different schemes, the highest amount of loan is Rs. 7796.60 lakhs in Uttar Pradesh, followed by Bihar with an amount of Rs. 4222.86 lakhs. The least amount released under different schemes in Meghalaya is Rs. 2.56 lakhs.

The above table depicts, under different schemes, IRDP, DRI and other schemes, the highest number of accounts having States are Uttar Pradesh and Bihar. In respect of amount released under the different schemes also Uttar Pradesh and Bihar occupy the first and the second place. The last place occupying States are Nagaland and Meghalaya.

REFINANCE OPERATIONS OF NABARD FOR RRBs TO SHORT-TERM OPERATIONS, 1989-90

The credit limits sanctioned to the Regional Rural Banks for financing Seasonal Agricultural Operations (SAO) and purposes

Table—3.8

Sanctioned Credit Limits to NABARD for RRBs Loans to State Governments

(Rs. in lakhs)

Particulars	*Year*	*Limits sanctioned*	*Repay-ments*	*Out-stan-dings*	*Drawals*
Short-Term Period Loans:					
At 3 per cent below and 5 per cent below bank rate from 1-3-1988 only for short-term agricultural operations and National Oil Seeds Development Project (SAO, NODP).	1986-87	22797	6018	20721	5312
	1987-88	30759	3782	27791	10852
	1988-89	36557	5910	34475	12594
Medium-Term Loans:					
1. Non-schematic (at 3 per cent below Bank rate).	1986-87	8032	3352	19926	9432
	1987-88	9931	3936	20308	4318
	1988-89	9438	2474	24039	6205
2. Covering of (ST) loans into (MT) loans at 3 per cent below Bank rate upto 29-8-1988 and 5 per cent below Bank rate from 1-3-1988 June-July, 1989.	1986-87	801	—	729	729
	1987-88	781	3	1395	669
	1988-89	476	416	1482	503

Source: NABARD Annual Report, 1990-91, pp. 140-141.

other than (SAO) recorded increase of more than 17 per cent over those of previous year; the reduction in the number of Banks availing the facility from 164 to 157. Credit limits sanctioned to RRBs Special Foodgrains Production Programme (SFPP) districts were 165 corers, forming 65 per cent of the total limits for (SAO) sanctioned to RRBs. Separate limits sanctioned under National Oil Seeds Development Project (NODP) recorded an impressive growth of about 61 per cent, despite a marginal reduction in the number of Banks availing such limits.

The amount of limits sanctioned was the highest in Andhra Pradesh (Rs. 98 crores sanctioned to 15 out of 16 RRBs) closely followed by Karnataka (77 crores to 13 RRBs). The Bank in Kerala appeared to be faring very well with two Banks accounting for the sanctioned limits of Rs. 54 crores. No credit limits were sanctioned to RRBs in Manipur, Nagaland, Arunachal Pradesh upto the end of March 1990. The performance of the Bihar also could not be considered as satisfactory, the limits sanctioned being only Rs. 8 crores to 8 Banks out of 22 Banks functioning in the State.

REGIONAL RURAL BANKS IN ANDHRA PRADESH

Despite the rapid increase in the number of Commercial Bank branches, especially after nationalisation, some districts are found deficient in terms of having Banking facilities. In order to meet effectively the Banking needs of people in un-Banked and under-Banked areas, Regional Rural Banks were established in Andhra Pradesh in the year 1976. The coverage and performance of RRBs in Andhra Pradesh are presented in Table—3.9.

The Regional Rural Banks made a beginning in Andhra Pradesh with the establishment of the first Regional Rural Bank on 30th April, 1976, Khammam and Nalgonda districts, christened "Nagarjuna Grameena Bank", sponsored by the State Bank of India. March 1991 it had 151 branches, Rs. 2464.23 lakhs of deposits in 2,99,157 accounts and outstanding credit of Rs. 4159.68 lakhs spread over 1,45,962 accounts, registering a credit deposit ratio of 169 per cent.

Table—3.9
Bank-wise Distribution of offices, deposits, outstanding Advances and Overdues of RRBs (At the End of March, 1991) In Andhra Pradesh

(Rs. in lakhs)

Sl. No.	Name of the Grameena Bank	Date of establish-ment	No. of Districts covered	No. of branches	Deposits		Outstanding Credit		Overdue advances		% of overdues to out-standing advances	Credit deposit ratio (i)
					No. of accounts	Amount	No. of accounts	Amount	No. of accounts	Amount		
1.	Nagarjuna Gr. Bank	30.04.1976	2	151	299157	2464.23	145962	4159.68	77732	2341.48	56.30	169
2.	Rayalaseema "	06.08.1976	3	142	453383	4587.02	197409	7683.39	47463	1703.89	22.20	168
3.	Sri Visakha "	30.09.1976	3	168	455632	4470.57	281832	5967.33	106923	1060.43	17.80	133
4.	Sree Anantha "	01.11.1979	1	69	184901	1676.55	57625	2092.55	25058	754.18	36.60	125
5.	Sri Venkateswara"	22.03.1981	1	71	174697	1622.50	84990	2954.39	34678	790.79	26.80	182
6.	Sri Saraswathi "	30.,03.1982	1	69	70011	1149.74	53285	1119.50	19629	274.06	24.50	97
7.	Sangameswara "	31.03.1982	1	65	49353	976.18	62612	1522.35	11947	217.91	14.30	156
8.	Majeera "	31.03.1982	1	64	75408	1578.58	60916	2166.41	14720	195.32	9.00	137
9.	Pinakini "	11.06.1982	2	83	169327	2168.22	84576	2706.27	17792	394.04	14.60	125
10.	Kakatiya "	28.06.1982	1	43	45801	615.17	40263	955.45	20742	478.31	50.10	155
11.	Chaitanya "	25.03.1983	1	44	67570	849.53	30681	1028.03	10389	374.01	36.40	121
12.	Sree Sathavahana"	28.03.1983	1	42	37039	649.51	40831	1125.95	14781	271.70	24.10	173
13.	Golkonda "	15.02.1985	1	22	12827	659.86	11488	291.88	2207	33.00	11.30	112
14.	Sree Rama "	21.02.1985	1	24	21376	292.41	10616	387.54	709	9.50	2.50	133
15.	Kanakadurga "	28.03.1986	1	26	13886	145.91	5741	196.07	1886	44.93	22.90	134
16.	Godavari "	11.04.1987	2	19	11074	167.14	4421	142.98	644	5.36	3.80	86
	Total		23	1102	2141442	23673.12	1173248	34499.77	407300	8948.87	225.90	146

Source: Statistics on Regional Rural Banks, National Bank for Agricultural and Rural Development (Regional Rural Banks Division), March 1991, p. 10.

The Rayalaseema Grameena Bank sponsored by the Syndicate Bank was established on 6th August 1976 covering Cuddapah and Kurnool districts in full, and parts of Prakasam district. By June 1987, it raised its branches to 142; mobilised deposits to the tune of Rs. 4587.02 lakhs through 4,53,383 accounts. It had an outstanding credit of Rs. 7683.39 lakhs in 1,97,409 accounts and credit deposit ratio of 168 per cent.

Sri Visakha Grameena Bank sponsored by the State Bank of India covering Srikakulam, Vijayanagaram, and Visakhapatnam districts was the third of the Regional Rural Banks in Andhra Pradesh which came into existence on 30th September 1976. It topped the list of all RRBs in the State in the number of branches (168); deposits amount Rs. 4470.57 lakhs through 4,55,632 accounts and outstanding credit of Rs. 5967.33 lakhs with an accounts of 2,81,832. It had the credit-deposit ratio of 133 per cent.

The fourth Regional Rural Bank namely, Sree Ananta Grameena Bank was established on 1st November, 1979, after a gap of three years; sponsored by the Syndicate Bank which is the Lead Bank of the district. By March 1991, it had deposits Rs. 1676.35 lakhs in 1,84,901 accounts; outstanding credit of Rs. 2092.55 lakhs in 57,625 accounts covered through 69 branches. It had credit-deposit ratio of 125 per cent.

The next Regional Rural Bank that came into operation was Sree Venkateswara Grameena Bank, sponsored by Indian Bank, in Chittoor district which started functioning from 22nd March 1981. By March 1991, it had mobilised deposits Rs. 1622.50 lakhs with 1,74,697 accounts; outstanding credit of Rs. 2954.39 lakhs through 84,990 accounts. It had a credit-deposit ratio of 182 per cent.

The year 1982 witnessed the establishment of five more Regional Rural Banks; the highest in any one year in Andhra Pradesh. Three of these were started in March 1982, while remaining two were started in June 1982. Sri Saraswathi Grameena Bank sponsored by the State Bank of Hyderabad, covering Adilabad district and established on March 1982, had

69 branches at March 1991. While Sangameswara Grameena Bank and Manjeera Grameena Bank, both sponsored by the State Bank of India and established on 31st March 1982, covered Mahaboobnagar and Medak districts respectively with 65 and 64 branches. Pinakini Grameena Bank started on 11th June 1982, sponsored by the Syndicate Bank with operation at Nellore and parts of Prakasam district. It had raised 83 branches. Kakatiya Grameena Bank, established by the State Bank of India on 28th June 1982 had Warangal district its operation area with 43 branches in 1991.

Next, two Regional Rural banks viz., Chaitanya and Sathavahana Grameena Bank, were established by Andhra Bank and the State Bank of Hyderabad, on 25th and 28th March 1983, respectively. By the end of March 1991, the former had 44 branches while the latter 42 branches.

The last four Regional Rural Banks to come into existence were Golkonda Grameena Bank, covering Hyderabad, established on 15th February 1985; Sree Rama Grameena Bank established on 21st February 1985 in Nizamabad district; Kanakadurga Grameena Bank (established on 28 March 1986 in Krishna district), Godavari Grameena Bank established on 11th April 1987 covering East and West Godavari districts. While the former two were sponsored by the State Bank of Hyderabad, the latter two were sponsored by the Indian Bank and Andhra Bank respectively. By March 1991, the four Regional Rural Banks operated through 22, 24, 26 and 19 branches respectively. The deposits mobilised by each of these Regional Rural Banks and their outstanding advances can be seen from Table—3.9.

The Table 3.10 *(See on page 62-63)* reveals purpose-wise disbursement of advances of Regional Rural Banks in Andhra Pradesh at the end of March 1991. Out of the total outstanding advances of Rs. 34499.77 lakhs of all RRBs in Andhra Pradesh, indirect advances amount of Rs. 752.27 lakhs (2.18 per cent). Agriculture and allied activities outstanding advances of Rs. 2419.90 lakhs (7.09 per cent) under 2,05,754 accounts. While non-agriculture rural artisans and village and cottage industries accounted for only 2,32,498 accounts, non-agriculture accounted for only Rs. 3010.56 lakhs (8.72 per cent). Agricultural sector received less priority than the non-agricultural sector.

Sri Rayalaseema Grameena Bank registered the highest figure of outstanding advances, Rs. 7683.39 lakhs, followed by Sri Visakha Grameena Bank, Rs. 5967.33 lakhs, Sri Venkateswara Grameena Bank, Rs. 2954.39 lakhs. The outstanding advances of all Regional Rural Banks in the State have been increasing year after year.

The Regional Rural Banks in Andhra Pradesh issued the amount under different schemes can be shown in Table—3.11. *(See on page 64)* Rayalaseema Grameena Bank is having the highest number of accounts under the Integrated Rural Development Programme is 8498. Out of the total accounts in Regional Rural Banks of Andhra Pradesh (24.5 per cent) are being with Rayalaseema Grameena Bank, followed by Sri Visakha Grameena Bank, having the number of accounts under IRDP 8189. This forms 23.6 per cent of the total accounts of Andhra Pradesh. The least number of accounts having under IRDP 67 is Godavari Grameena Bank. Out of the total accounts, RRBs in Andhra Pradesh (6.35 per cent), is the least number of accounts having under Integrated Rural Development Programme.

As far as the amount issued, Visakha Grameena Bank is leading other Grameena Banks Rs. 600.53 lakhs (42.63 per cent) under Integrated Rural Development Programme, followed by Rayalaseema Grameena Bank having issued Rs. 224.64 lakhs (15.94 per cent) under Integrated Rural Development Programme. The least amount Rs. 0.43 lakhs are issued by the Godavari Grameena Bank under IRDP scheme. This is the 0.31 percentage of the total amount issued under IRDP.

Under Differential Rate of Interest scheme, (DRI) Rayalaseema Grameena Bank is having the highest number of accoutns 391 (71.6 per cent) under Integrated Rural Development Programme. This is followed by Pinakini Grameena Bank 118 (21.61 per cent).

Table—3.10
Bank-wise, purpose-wise classification of advances of Regional Rural Banks (at the end of March, 1991)

Rs. in Lakhs

Sl. No.	Name of the Grameena Bank	Name of the spon-sored Bank	Direct Advances: Short-term Crop loans		Teran loans: Agricultural investments		Teran loans: Allied activities		Rural artisans Village and Cottage Indus-tries	
			No. of accounts	Amount	No. of accounts	Amount	No. of accounts	Amount	No. of accounts	Amount
1.	Nagarguna Gr. Bank	SBI	36626	937.42	17765	637.27	7286	171.44	8810	102.20
2.	Rayalaseena Gr. Bank	Syndicate Bank	104542	4278.51	11388	540.44	16524	501.43	11468	214.66
3.	Sri Visakha Gr. Bank	SBI	73440	1321.57	28827	666.67	23585	545.46	11431	272.51
4.	Sree Anantha Gr. Bank	Syndicate	23018	797.30	6764	518.60	3617	148.30	7542	192.22
5.	Sree Vankateswara Gr. Bank	Indian	45967	1579.77	8447	311.62	7375	239.37	3940	49.38
6.	Sri Saraswathi Gr. Bank	SBH	25235	492.16	10443	330.80	1102	25.70	3701	43.82
7.	Sangameswara Gr. Bank	SBI	26830	708.48	5181	253.43	3960	109.12	7236	109.95
8.	Manjeera Gr. Bank	SBI	32653	998.96	6275	481.41	4894	142.39	3540	123.76
9.	Pinakini Gr. Bank	Syndicate	31892	1118.96	6163	246.46	7513	246.65	3127	70.81
10.	Kakatiya Gr. Bank	SBI	20844	461.77	3534	117.75	1663	55.41	1369	17.67
11.	Chaitanya Gr. Bank	Andhra	13774	557.03	4559	183.28	2095	41.87	178	4.58
12.	Sathavahana Gr. Bank	SBH	17835	502.72	8200	291.66	2726	89.65	2554	41.18
13.	Golkonda Gr. Bank	SBH	5282	123.75	1304	55.80	1273	44.88	824	16.16
14.	Sri Rama Gr. Bank	SBH	5771	197.00	969	89.98	1013	34.61	122	2050
15.	Kanakadurga Gr. Bank	Indian	3766	146.78	205	5.31	535	16.80	8	0.15
16.	Godavari Gr. Bank	Andhra	1577	61.79	87	9.48	209	6.82	12	0.45
	Total		470052	14583.97	120084	4739.96	85676	2419.90	65862	1261.37

(Table Contd... .)

(Table 3.10 Contd. ...)

Sl. No.	Name of the Grameena Bank	Direct Advances						Indirect advances		Total outstanding advances		Balances with Bank
		Retail Trade/ Small Business self-employed etc.		Consumption loans		Other purposes						
		No. of accounts	Amount	No. of accounts	Amount	No. of accounts	Amount	No. of accounts	Amount	No. of accounts	Amount	Amount
1.	Nagarguna Gr. Bank	15869	254.16	–	–	59476	1960.06	132	97.14	145962	4159.68	736.8
2.	Rayalaseena Gr. Bank	31204	725.77	371	1.78	20836	770.57	1076	650.25	197409	7683.39	1775.5
3.	Sri Visakha Gr. Bank	40001	331.02	7841	210.19	96707	2619.91	–	–	281832	5967.33	2070.4
4.	Sree Anantha Gr. Bank	8715	250.97	5415	144.00	1554	41.16	–	–	57625	2092.55	1099.5
5.	Sree Vankateswara Gr. Bank	10191	175.38	–	–	9098	248.79	2	0.08	84990	2954.39	544.0
6.	Sri Saraswathi Gr. Bank	8962	100.10	–	–	2842	118.92	–	–	53285	1119.50	634.4
7.	Sangameswara Gr. Bank	10996	162.11	246	1.55	8163	177.71	–	–	62612	1522.35	454.0
8.	Manjeera Gr. Bank	10897	279.63	–	–	2656	135.50	1	4.76	60916	2166.41	1206.0
9.	Pinakini Gr. Bank	6579	150.88	5	0.02	29297	873.17	–	–	84576	2706.27	687
10.	Kakatiya Gr. Bank	3928	65.03	1662	55.04	7263	182.78	–	–	40263	955.45	260
11.	Chaitanya Gr. Bank	4508	73.72	3	0.28	5564	167.32	–	–	30681	1028.03	549
12.	Sathavahana Gr. Bank	7885	141.06	1502	51.57	179	8.11	–	–	40831	1125.95	365
13.	Golkonda Gr. Bank	2553	43.06	–	–	252	8.23	–	–	11488	291.88	187
14.	Sri Rama Gr. Bank	1887	43.34	–	–	554	20.11	–	–	10616	387.54	176
15.	Kanakadurga Gr. Bank	970	18.72	–	–	254	8.31	–	–	5741	196.07	54
16.	Godavari Gr. Bank	1543	25.30	10	1.42	983	36.72	–	–	4421	142.98	185
	Total	166636	2849.19	18055	465.74	245678	7427.37	1211	752.27	1173248	34499.77	10953

Source: Statistics on Regional Rural Banks (NABARD), Regional Rural Bank Division, March, 1991, pp. 32-33.

Table—3.11

Bank-wise Loans Issued Under Special Programmes from April 1990 to March 1991

(Rs. in lakhs)

Sl. No.	Name of the Grameena Bank	IRDP		DRI		Others		Total	
		No. of Accounts	Amount	No. of Accounts	Amount	No. of Accounts	Amount	No. of Accounts	Amount
1.	Nagarjuna	1409	25.92	–	–	–	–	1409	25.92
2.	Rayalaseema	8498	224.64	391	4.08	2748	89.36	11367	318.08
3.	Sri Visakha	8189	600.53	–	–	113	4.73	8302	605.26
4.	Sree Anantha	3948	143.87	12	0.23	598	20.49	4558	166.59
5.	Sri Venkateswara	3119	100.82	–	–	1887	54.31	5006	155.13
6.	Sri Saraswathi	1189	30.76	–	–	165	16.71	1294	47.47
7.	Sangameswara	312	9.12	–	–	112	2.54	424	11.66
8.	Manjeera	1639	52.75	–	–	–	–	1639	52.75
9.	Pinakini	2122	67.80	118	0.01	22502	783.12	24742	850.93
10.	Kakatiya	93	3.90	–	–	26	0.88	119	4.78
11.	Chaitanya	576	19.19	19	0.06	36	1.02	631	20.27
12.	Sree Sathavahana	1617	55.58	–	–	399	18.02	2016	73.60
13.	Golkonda	1043	31.11	–	–	476	14.97	1519	46.08
14.	Sri Rama	455	29.69	–	–	–	–	455	29.69
14.	Kanakadurga	405	12.46	6	0.22	–	–	411	12.68
16.	Godavari	67	0.43	–	–	428	8.13	40	8.56
	Total	34621	1408.57	546	4.60	29485	1014.28	64652	2427.45

Source: Statistics on Regional Rural Banks (NABARD) Regional Rural Banks Division, March 1992, p. 58.

The amount of loans issued under Differential Rate of Interest scheme, Rayalaseema Grameena Bank issued highest amount Rs. 4.08 (88.69 per cent), which is followed by Sree Anantha Grameena Bank amount Rs. 0.23 lakhs (5 per cent). The least amount issued under DRI scheme, Rs. 0.01 lakhs, is Pinakini Grameena Bank.

Kakatiya Grameena Bank is having the highest number of accoutns under various schemes, 24,742, with an amount of Rs. 4.78 lakhs; whereas Sri Visakha Grameena Bank with 11,637 accounts, with an amount of extended loans to the extent of Rs. 605.26 lakhs, is the least. Manjeera Grameena Bank occupied the first place in the issue of loans under various schemes with an amount of Rs. 850.93 lakhs.

DANTWALA COMMITTEE RECOMMENDATIONS

The Reserve Bank of India appointed in June 1977 a committee "to review the working of Regional Rural Banks" under the Chairmanship of Prof. M.L. Dantwala. The Review Committee was assigned the work to evaluate the performance of Regional Rural Banks in the light of the objectives for which they were set up; to indicate their precise role in the rural credit structure and to make recommendations with regard to the scope, methods and procedures of their functioning and other matters of enquiry. After reviewing the overall progress of the business of all the RRBs functioning in the country upto the end of June 1977, the Dantwala Committee submitted its report to the Reserve Bank on February 1978. The Reserve Bank announced its decisions on the major recommendations of the Review Committee Report on RRBs in September 1978.

The Dantwala Committee was convinced that, within a short period of two years, RRBs have demonstrated their capability to serve the purpose for which they were established. The RRBs have established their image as a new type of institution, catering to the credit-needs of a class of borrowers to whom institutional-credit was hitherto unavailable. With some modifications in their organisation and functioning, the RRBs can become a very useful component in the totality of rural credit structure. The Committee felt that the RRBs could make substantial contribution towards improving the quality and quantity of credit, so as to do justice to the local people and their problems, by shortcoming the existing jurisdiction which is unduly large. The Committee opined that "the jurisdiction of a rural bank is confined to one district" since the size and state of economic development of districts vary a great deal. It is wise to retain some flexibility in this and other related matters. One RRB is expected to cover a population of 10 to 15 lakhs. From the angle of financial viability and managerial efficiency, the reasonable number of branches per district should be between 50 and 60. This would mean that "one Regional Rural Bank branch would be enough approximately for a population of above 20,000 and an area roughly equal to that covered by five recognised primary agricultural credit societies."

The Review Committee did not recommend any change in the authorised and paid-up capital of an RRB from the present level. It recommended certain changes, however in the composition of share capital. It endorsed the need for local participation by Co-operatives, other local institutions and individuals in the share capital of RRBs and also for paying a minimum guaranteed divided to such share holders at the rate which was recommended earlier by the Narasimham working group. This was suggested as there were distinct advantages in permitting local participation in the share capital of RRBs. In case of a shortfall in the share of the local participation, it may be filled up by the sponsoring Bank or the Reserve Bank of India with the provision that, as and when local demand for subscription comes up, the shares so held may be released to the eligible institutions and individuals. It further suggested that "hereafter the RBI instead of the Central Government may contribute to the share capital". Similarly the Committee argued the case for increasing the share of the sponsoring Bank in the share capital of RRBs by 5 per cent over the present level. The composition of the share capital of a RRB recommended by the Review Committee was as follows:

Reserve Bank of India	25 per cent
Sponsoring Bank	40 per cent

State Government	15 per cent
Local participation	20 per cent

The Committee recommended that the Board of each RRB should consist of 9 members including Chairman of the remaining Directors, they should be nominated by the sponsoring Bank. One by Reserve Bank of India, two by the State Government and two to be nominated by Reserve Bank of India from amongst the local shareholders.

The Committee emphasised that RRBs are supposed to be established in the areas where existing credit facilities are inadequate, the Commission suggested that a dominant share (60 per cent) of total loans be reserved by the RRBs for the weaker sections and the remaining (upto 40 per cent) may be lent to large farmers and other borrowers, not covered by these Banks at present. The Committee also recommended that the RRBs be allowed to offer full Banking facilities especially because of its view that the rural branches of Commercial Banks are not to operate in the areas served by RRBs.

The Committee, therefore, recommended the establishments of RRBs especially in those areas were the DCCBs were unable to fully meet the credit needs of the farming in the district through the primary agricultural credit societies.

On the basis of the recommendations of the Dantwala Committee, the Reserve Bank of India opined that the Regional Rural Banks had very important role to play in the sphere of rural credit. In assisting weaker sections and in the upliftment of the rural poor, RRBs have been actively working and designing various plans since then. They provide financial assistance to identified borrowers under 20 Point Programme, IRDP, and other programmes planned for the upliftment of Scheduled Castes and Scheduled Tribes. They operate the Differential Rate of Interest scheme on agency basis and, therefore, they seem to fulfil another criterion, namely efficient and equitable deployment of credit in different rural areas and for different class of borrowers.[11]

KELKAR WORKING GROUP'S RECOMMENDATIONS

The Government of India set up a working group under the Chairmanship of Sri. V.K. Das in August 1984 (further it is under Chairmanship of S.M. Kelkar) to go into the various aspects of the functioning of RRBs and make suitable recommendations for further policy. The review was felt necessary in the context of a large number of Regional Rural Banks (at that time 188) being established in the country and in view of certain weakness discernible in the working results of RRBs, particularly relating to their profitability aspect. The working group examined the data in respect of 188 RRBs established until 1985 and arrived at certain conclusions. The group was convinced, taking into consideration the average size of deposits (Rs. 712) and loans per account (Rs. 1886), that these Banks have catered successfully to the Banking requirements of small men in rural areas of the country.

The group felt that the Regional Rural Banks, as a part of multi-agency approach to rural credit, are eminently suitable to do the job particularly in view of its large branch network, comparatively lower cost of operation, local involvement and operations in tune with the national objectives of serving the weaker sections. They can be trusted as district level organisations, to take Banking closer to the rural households and ensure effective supervision over the end-use of credit. They can co-exist along side of the co-operatives and Commercial Banks, playing a supplementary role to each other.

The working group referred to the new-branch licensing policy of the RBI for the Seventh Plan period and recommended relaxation in respect of RRBs, taking into account the need and viability aspects. The new licensing policy envisaged the Block as 'a unit' and that a branch would cover 200 sq. km. area. Under this policy, fresh licences would be issued only in deficit Blocks which do not conform to the above norms. The group felt that once a Regional Rural Bank is required to be established in an area, viability considerations demand that sufficient number of branches should be allowed to be opened by it and so the need for RBI to relax the policy makers on the merits of each cases. The group also recommended that priority may be continued to be given to RRBs while issuing licences for rural areas.

Regarding the authorised and paid up share capital of RRBs, the group felt that there was a case for increasing the share capital by a substantial amount in view of increasing number of branches of RRBs and the escalation of costs over the years. The existing paid-up share capital of Rs. 25 lakhs provide a very limited capital-base to the RRBs. The group recommended that the composition of Board, apart from the Chairman should be as follows:

Government of India	:	2 Non-officials
Reserve Bank of India	:	1 official
NABARD	:	1 official
Sponsor Bank	:	2 officials
State Government	:	2 officials

Further, the group felt that the respective nominating authorities have to be allowed to nominate their officers directly, without any reference to Government of India and without the Government of India following the present procedure of issuing notification nominating the various persons on the Board representing sponsor Bank and State Government which is unnecessary and time consuming. Similarly, the Chairman to be appointed directly by the sponsor Bank in consultation with NABARD. Sufficiently-senior officers of sponsor Bank with organisational experience at its Head Office in management of funds, human resources and industrial relations etc., and having been imparted preferably a suitable orientation training programme should be selected by sponsor Bank for being appointed as Chairman.

In conclusion, the group observed that the various measures suggested by them have to be accepted and implemented as a package and not in isolation. The recommendations, if properly implemented, the group felt, would make RRBs more effective and better-equipped institutions to subserve the rural-weak which was the primary objective for their establishment.

No doubt, the multi-agency approach, and the co-operative system have achieved what was expected of them i.e., rural development. Further the Banks in India deserve commendation for the extra-ordinary achievement they have achieved since the Day of Nationalisation in terms of their services for rural development. While accepting the challenges and meeting the same, there are some internal problems faced by the Commercial Banks, resulting in the lack of proper house-keeping, slackening control, delay in collecting instruments, deterioration customer service and monitoring public criticism.

It might be right to mention here the great need of the time is to have greater integrated approach of all the agencies involved in the rural-credit delivery system.

All the plans and policies, formulated and implemented so far, placed emphasis on the quantitative credit expansion. Thinking on the role of credit is undergoing a change among a school of economists, shifting emphasis from quantity to quality, considering credit as a finance-created by financial market rather than an input responding to the market needs.

In the ultimate analysis, it can be said that, although micro-level planning provides essential base for Integrated Rural Development (IRD), it would be an illusion to expect far more from the existing system than what it is providing today.

If the financial agencies follow an innovative approach, if pursuing the goal of bringing social and economical transformation in the society, solving the problems of poverty and unemployment certainly becomes easier. Taking into consideration the enormative content with what has been done so far, the challenge to financial institutions will continue increasingly for many more years to come before they could possibly claim that they have done all that is possible within the limitations of their resources.

REFERENCE

1. Reserve Bank of India, *'The General Report of the All India Rural Credit Survey Committee'*, 1954, Bombay, p. 8.

2. *'Agricultural Credit in Asia'*, Report on *Regional Seminar for Asia on Agricultural Credit for Small Farmers held at Bangkok, Thailand,* October 1974, (FAO).

3. National Commission on Agriculture Interim Report on *"Credit Service of Small and Marginal Farmers and Agricultural Labourers"*, New Delhi, 1971, p. 569.

4. Government of India, *'Report of Banking Commission'*, 1972, pp. 165-174.

5. Guglani, P.L., and Pandey, R.K., *"Financing the Neglected Sector—Agriculture"*, Yojana, July, 1983, p. 21.

6. *Ibid.*, pp. 21-22.

7. Narasimham, M., was the Additional Secretary in the Department of Economic Affairs, Government of India.

8. Government of India, *the Regional Rural Banks Act, 1976,* Ministry of Law and Justice and Company Affairs, New Delhi, 1976, p. 21.

9. *Ibid.*, p. 21.

10. Mello, L.D., *"Lead Bank Scheme and Role of Rural Banks—State Bank of India"*, Economic Review, February 1976, p. 70.

11. Reserve Bank of India, *'All India Rural Credit Survey'*, Report of the Committee of Direction, 1988, Vol. 2, p. 54.

Chapter—4

Rayalaseema Grameena Bank

1. Brief History of the Bank

Rayalaseema Grameena Bank was established on 6.8.1976 with its Head Office at Cuddapah in the State of Andhra Pradesh, under the RRB act, 1976. Rayalaseema Grameena Bank is one among the 10 RRBs sponsored by Syndicate Bank. The Area of operation of the bank covers three districts—entire Cuddapah and Kurnool Districts and Markapur Revenue Division of Prakasam district. The Bank is catering to the needs of 982 Service Area Villages in 3 districts. The Bank had successfully implemented prudential accounting norms and geared up itself for the new challenges well. The Bank is actively participating in Developmental Programmes of Government in providing credit to the poor and needy persons.

The soils of the area are mainly black and red. The rivers flowing in the area are Penna, Papagni, Cheyyeru, Sagileru, Pincha, Bahuda, Chitravati, Kundu, Tungabhadra, Handri, Krishna, Gundlakamma etc. The irrigation projects benefitting the area are Kurnool-Cuddapah Canal, Tungabhadra Project Low Level Canal, Tungabhadra Project High Level Canal, Srisailam Right Branch Canal, Telugu Ganga Canal, Pincha Project, Sagileru Project, Gajuladinne and Mylavaram Reservoirs.

The Principal Crops grown in the area are: Paddy, Jowar, Groundnut, Seed Jowar, Seed Cotton, Sunflower, Commercial Cotton, Chillies, Coriander and Onions. Kurnool district is a major seed producer in Andhra Pradesh and it ranks first among the district in respect of jowar and cotton hybrid seeds. Cuddapah and Kurnool districts are rich in minerals such as limestone, asbestos, barytes, granites, black and colour slabs etc.

Most of the area of operation was severely affected by drought during the year. The rain fall during the year in Cuddapah district was 454.4 mm as against district normal rain fall of 696 mm and in Kurnool district it was 491.1 mm as against normal rain fall of 630 mm and in markapur division of Prakasam district it was 638 mm as against normal rain fall of 666.8 mm. The Bank had instructed the branches to rephase short-term loans besides extending fresh finance in drought affected areas.

2. Branch Net Work

The Bank has 140 Branches, consisting of 106 Rural, 23 semi urban and 11 urban branches besides 7 Area Offices. The Bank has also sponsored 8 Farmers Service Societies.

Spread of Branch Net Work

District	*No. of Branches*	*Rural*	*Semi Urban*	*Urban*	*Area Offices*	*FSCCs*	*Extension counters*
Cuddapah	66	52	9	5	3	4	-
Kurnool	59	44	9	6	3	4	-
Prakasam	15	10	5	-	1	-	-
Total	140	106	23	11	7	8	-

3. Share Capital

The authorised and paid up capital of the Bank are Rs. 50000 thousands and Rs. 10000 thousands respectively. The Government of India under restructuring programme of RRBs in Phase-II during 1996-97, approved provision of additional liquidity support amounting Rs. 147511 thousands to cleanse the balance sheet. The contributions made by the share holders are furnished in the following table.

(Rs. in thousands)

Contributors	*Share Capital*	*Share Capital Deposit Account*
Government of India	5000	73755.60
Syndicate Bank	3500	51628.90
Govt. of Andhra Pradesh	1500	22126.50
Total	10000	147511.00

4. Deposits

The total deposits of the Bank, as at the end of March 2000 stood at Rs. 3678799 thousands against the MoU target of Rs. 3600000 thousands. The net accretion in deposits during the year is Rs. 654114 thousands. Registering a growth rate of 21.63% as against 15.58% of last year. The growth in average deposits is 22.81% as against 20.65% of last year.

The total demand deposits of the bank stood at Rs. 897274 thousands as on 31.03.2000 compared to the previous year level of Rs. 827653 thousands constituting 24.41% total deposits. The composition of deposits is shown in the following table.

Composition of Deposits as on 31.3.2000

(Rs. in thousands)

S. No.	*Type of Deposit*		*Accounts*	*Amount*	*% to total deposits*
	1		*2*	*3*	*4*
1.	**Demand Deposits**				
	(a)	Current Accounts	2752	54382	1.48
	(b)	Savings Bank	489137	804897	21.88
	(c)	Others	51650	38629	105
		Total	543539	897908	24.41

(Contd. ...)

1		2	3	4
2.	**Time Deposits**			
(a)	Fixed Deposits	12095	314796	8.56
(b)	Cumulative (Recurring) Deposit	10385	54593	1.48
(c)	Janakalpa Deposit	24307	64347	1.75
(d)	Lakshmi Cash Certificate	45083	808483	21.98
(e)	Ishwarya Cash Certificate	57701	1234040	33.54
(f)	Bhagya Cash Certificate	621	11156	0.30
(g)	Janabhadratha deposit	2573	80092	2.18
(h)	Kamadhenu Deposit	335	9364	0.25
(i)	Karshakamitra Deposit	17758	32682	0.89
(j)	Samraksha	430	406	0.01
(k)	Others	8138	170932	4.65
	Total	179426	2780891	75.59
	Grand Total (1+2)	722965	3678799	100.00

The average cost of deposits worked out to 9.03% during the year under report as against 9.05% of the preceding year. The per employee deposits recorded an increase of Rs. 690 thousands and stood at Rs. 3824 thousands as against Rs. 3134 thousands of preceding year. The per branch deposits has increased to a level of Rs. 26277 thousands from a previous year level of Rs. 21605 thousands.

5. Borrowings

The Bank has been availing refinance from NABARD, Sponsor Bank and SIDBI on eligible loans and advances. The Bank had drawn refinance to the tune of Rs. 669219 thousands during the year. The scheme-wise and agency-wise details of Refinance limits sanctioned, limits utilised, refinance drawn, repaid and outstanding are given in the below table.

Scheme-wise Details of Refinance

(Rs. in thousands)

Institution/Scheme	Position of Refinance Limits			Position of Refinance	
	Sanctioned	Utilised	Drawn	Repaid	Outstanding
(A) NABARD					
ST-SAO	143600	143600	143600	174056	143600
ST-OPP	262300	262300	262300	288408	262300
ST-DTP	4200	4200	4200	4228	4200
ST-OSAO	800	715	658	912	658
MT-(Schematic)	43000	34194	34194	46686	103869
MT-(Non-Schematic)	–	–	–	4269	–
MT-(Con)	–	–	–	7327	6278
Total	453900	445009	444952	525886	520905
(B) Sponsor Bank					
ST-OPP	136800	136800	136800	127796	136849
ST-DTP & OTM	88400	80741	84646	72481	81636
ST-OSAO	600	389	389	509	250
ST-(Non-Schematic)	–	–	–	6235	1431
MT-(Con)	–	–	–	2294	2833
Total	225800	217930	221835	209405	222999
(C) SIDBI (ARS)	4000	2432	2432	13811	20814
GRAND TOTAL	683700	665371	669219	749102	764718

The average cost of Borrowings during the year under report is worked out to 7.66%. The Bank has kept up its regular repayment record in respect of commitments to refinancing agencies throughout the year.

6. Other Liabilities

The Bank has opted out from the DICGC coverage both from Small Loan Guarantee Scheme (SLGS) 1971 and Small Scale Industries (1981) Scheme and withdrew participation with effect from 1.4.1995. The particulars of claims lodged, settled and pending with DICGC as on 31.3.2000 and for the past 2 years are furnished below.

DICGC Claims (Cumulative)

(Rs. in thousands)

Particulars	*1997-98*		*1998-99*		*1999-2000*	
	Accounts	*Amount*	*Accounts*	*Amount*	*Accounts*	*Amount*
Claims Lodged	83256	236020	83256	236020	83256	236020
Claims Settled	78688	218961	79644	221990	82545	232970
Claims pending for settlement	4568	17059	3612	14030	711	3050

7. Cash and Balances with Banks

The cash balances held by the bank as on 31.3.2000 was Rs. 50037 thousands and the average cash balance held during the year was Rs. 25931 thousands. The particulars of cash balance, average cash balance, the balance with Reserve Bank of India and other commercial banks as on 31.3.2000 and for the past two years are furnished hereunder.

(Rs. in thousands)

Sl. No.	*Particulars*	*1997-98*	*1998-99*	*1999-2000*
1.	Cash in Hand	56799	67744	50041
2.	Average Cash Balance	16745	21372	25931
3.	Average Cash Deposit Ratio	0.85	0.90	0.80
4.	Balances in RBI Account	72276	94166	99424
5.	Balances held by the Bank with Sponsor Bank	91695	15694	8385
6.	Balance with other Commercial Banks	72858	56060	34828
7.	Income Earned on Bank Balances			
	(a) with Sponsor Bank	3377	658	–
	(b) with Commercial Banks	875	265	–

The income earned on Bank balances with Sponsor Bank and with other Scheduled Commercial Banks during the year 1999-2000 is-NIL-as all the banks including Sponsor Bank have discontinued payment of interest on balances in Current Account with effect from 1.10.1998.

8. Investments

The total investments of the Bank stood at Rs. 2244279 thousands as on 31.3.2000 as against the previous year level of Rs. 1739039 thousands. The particulars of investments held under approved securities and other securities as well as under SLR and Non-SLR are furnished in the below table.

(Rs. in thousands)

S. No.	*Type of Investment*	*31.3.1999*	*31.3.2000*
1.	Approved Securities	132500	104214
2.	Other Securities	–	–
3.	SLR	688093	859582
4.	Non-SLR	770935	1280483
5.	Share Capital Deposit	147511	–
6.	Interest Earned on Investments		
	(*a*) SLR	81304	94701
	(*b*) Non-SLR	99393	135194

The Average yield on SLR investments during the year 1999-2000 is 11.29% as against previous year yield of 12.17%. The average return on Non-SLR investments during the year 1999-2000 is 11.49% as against previous return of 12.48%.

9. Loans and Advances Outstanding

Even though various package of measures and relaxations have been accorded by Government of India for strengthening the Regional Rural Banks, the Bank has not neglected the target group and ensured its uninterrupted flow of credit to them. The total outstanding advances stood at Rs. 2630881 thousands as at the end of March 2000 as against previous year level of Rs. 2416314 thousands, registering a growth rate of 8.88%. The Sector-wise classification of advances as at the end of March 1999 and March 2000 are shown in the following table.

(Rs. in thousands)

S. No.	Sector	31.3.1999		31.3.2000	
		Accounts	*Amounts*	*Accounts*	*Amount*
1.	Agriculture				
	(a) Direct	114171	1260130	113808	1471561
	(b) Indirect	429	47037	259	53351
2.	Small Scale Industries	8808	46740	7131	38827
3.	Small Business	18357	118177	15941	110068
4.	Transport Operators	931	55859	694	40946
5.	Business Enterprises	4978	39122	4050	32116
6.	Professional & Sell employed	4572	25485	3570	22696
7.	Self Help Groups	—	—	209	3550
	Priority Sector	152246	1592550	145662	1773115
	% to Total Advances		65.91		67.40
	Non-Priority Sector	82334	823764	85979	857766
	% to Total Advances		34.09		32.60
	Total	234580	2416314	231641	2630881

The per branch Advances stood at Rs. 18792 thousand as against previous year's position of Rs. 17259 thousands.

The Credit Deposit Ratio is 71.51% as against previous year 79.88%.

10. Income Recognition and Asset Classification Norms

(a) Asset Classification

As per Reserve Bank of India directives the Bank had adopted the prudential and Asset Classification Norms from the year 1995-96. The amount outstanding under Non-Performing Assets (NPAs) as on 31.3.2000 is Rs. 401457 thousands constituting 15.26% against Gross Advances as against the corresponding figure of Rs. 483617 thousands as on 31.3.1999, constituting 20% against Gross Advances. The detailed classification of Assets as on 31.3.2000 and 31.3.1999 are furnished below.

NPAS Position as at 31.3.1999 and 31.3.2000

(Rs. in thousands)

Asset Category	*31.3.1999*			*31.3.2000*		
	Amount Outstanding as on 31.3.1999	*% of share to total advances*	*Provision*	*Amount outstanding as on 31.03.2000*	*% of share to total advances*	*Provision*
Standard	1932697	80	—	2229424	84.74	5574
Sub-Standard	116653	5	11665	81951	3.11	8195
Doubtful	290540	12	105638	254399	9.67	95577
Loss	76424	3	44641	65107	2.48	46892
Total	2416314	100	161944	2630881	100.00	156238

(b) Interest De-recognised

The quantum of interest de-recognised during the current year as well as previous year and also the amount realised against the derecognised interest are furnished below.

Derecognised Interest

(Rs. in thousands)

Particulars	*31.3.1999*	*31.3.2000*
Derecognised income at the beginning of the year	123200	170570
Recovery during the year	45000	46664
Additions during the year	92370	90114
Derecognised income at the end of the year	170570	214020

(c) Provisions

The total provisions held by the Bank and the provisions held against NPAs for current year as well as for the past two years are furnished in the following table.

(Rs. in thousands)

Particulars	*1997-98*	*1998-99*	*1999-2000*
Provision against NPAs	173011	161944	156238
Others (frauds, theft etc.)	671	574	716
Total	173682	162518	156954

(d) NPA Management

The Sub-standard, Doubtful and Loss assets as at the end of current year and previous year are furnished below.

NPAs Position

(Rs. in thousands)

Particulars		*31.3.1999*	*31.3.2000*
(a)	NPAs at the beginning of the year	542100	483617
(b)	Recovery against NPAs during the year	128224	166454
(c)	Addition to NPAs during the year	69741	84295
(d)	NPAs at the end of the year	483617	401457
	Net NPAs (NPA-Provisions)	321673	245219
	Net Advances (Gross Advances—Provisions)	2254370	2474643

11. Loan Disbursements

During the year under report the Bank has disbursed Rs. 1942324 thousands under all Sectors of Credit as against Rs. 1767074 thousand of 1999. The comparative position of purpose-wise, sector-wise disbursements are furnished in the following table.

Comparative Position of Purpose-wise Disbursements

(Rs. in thousands)

	Purpose	1998-99		1999-2000	
		Accounts	Amount	Accounts	Amount
1.	Crop Production	60651	645600	66891	844941
2.	Minor Irrigation	113	2395	43	980
3.	Land Development	25	506	19	787
4.	Bullock & Carts	66	808	47	653
5.	Agricultural Tractors	32	7127	42	10069
6.	Horticulture	13	110	1	255
7.	Other Term Loans	17	249	9	129
8.	Dairy Units	377	4338	176	2058
9.	Sheep Units	358	4086	202	2649
10.	Sericutlrue	43	563	16	215
11.	Other Allied Activities	36	715	5	230
12.	SSI Rural Artisans	1087	7515	1039	7351
13.	Small Business & Business Enterprises	7875	79569	7477	76186
14.	Transport Operators	122	11505	133	11690
15.	Professional & Self Employed	594	5318	625	6449
16.	Self Help Groups	—	—	174	3586
17.	Others	97193	958721	87712	929201
18.	Indirect Finance through FSCS	253	37949	195	44895
	Total	168855	1767074	164806	1942324

Of the total disbursements, lion's share i.e. 43% has gone for crop production and 3.92% has gone to Small Business.

Comparative Position of Sector-wise Disbursements During 1999-2000 and 1998-99

(Rs. in thousands)

	Sector	*1998-99*		*1999-2000*	
		Accounts	*Amounts*	*Accounts*	*Amounts*
1.	Agriculture				
	(a) Direct	61731	666497	67451	862966
	(b) Indirect	253	37949	195	44895
2.	Small Scale Industries	1087	7515	1039	7351
3.	Small Business	4410	43889	4671	47825
4.	Transport Operators	122	11505	133	11690
5.	Business Enterprises	3465	35680	2806	28361
6.	Professional & Self Employed	594	5318	625	6449
7.	Self Help Groups	–	–	174	3586
	Priority	71662	808353	77094	1013123
	Non-Priority	97193	958721	87712	929201
	Total	168855	1767074	164806	1942324

Comparative Position of Share of Target and Non Target Groups During 1998-99 and 1999-2000

(Rs. in thousands)

	1998-99	*1999-2000*
Target Group	1041479	1234120
% in total	58.94	63.54
Non-Target Group	725595	708204
% in total	41.06	36.46
Total	1767074	1942324

Government Sponsored Schemes

The Bank has been implementing Integrated Rural Development Programme. Schedule Caste Action Plan (SCAP) and other Government Sponsored Poverty Alleviation Programmes to uplift and develop weaker sections. The particulars of targets and grounding under various Government Schemes are furnished below.

Disbursements Under Government Sponsored Schemes During the Year 1999-2000

(Rs. in thousands)

Scheme	*Target*		*Grounded*		*% of grounding*
	Units	*Amount*	*Units*	*Amount*	
1. IRDP/SGSY	1631	27409	1337	8055	82
2. SCAP	809	6199	157	1613	19
3. BCAP	1241	7330	57	519	5
4. Others	479	3936	0	784	19
Total	4160	44874	1641	10971	37

Annual Credit Plan

The bank continued to play its effective role in implementation of Annual Credit Plans in Cuddapah, Kurnool and Prakasam districts during 1999-2000. The achievements is 110.54% with Rs. 1942324 thousands as against the allocation of Rs. 1757122 thousands. The comparative position of allocation and achievements under Annual Credit Plans during 1998-99 and 1999-2000 is furnished below.

(Rs. in thousands)

District		*1998-99*			*1999-2000*		
	No. of Branches	*Allocation*	*Achievement*	*%*	*Allocation*	Achievement	%
Cuddapah	66	903530	918657	101.67	988200	989043	100.09
Kurnool	59	678058	728069	107.38	691045	826474	119.60
Prakasham	15	96075	120348	125.26	77877	126807	162.83
Total	140	1677663	1767074	105.33	1757122	1942324	110.54

12. Recovery of Loans

The Recovery percentage of the Bank as on 30.6.99 stood at 55%. During the year Bank has taken several measures to step up recoveries in general and Non-Performing Assets in particular. The DCB position of the bank for the current year vis-a-vis for previous two years is given in the following table.

DCB Position

(Rs. in thousands)

As at	*Demand*	*Collection*	*Balance*	*% of recoveries to demand*
June 1997	1483646	662796	820850	45%
June 1998	1174617	611673	562944	52%
June 1999	1741005	958580	782425	55%

The Particulars of age-wise and sector-wise overdues based on June 1999 DCB are given below:

(Rs. in thousands)

Sector	*Upto 1 year*	*1 year to 3 years*	*Above 3 years*	*Total*
Farm Sector	315405	140410	220913	676728
Non-Farm Sector	12708	29787	63202	105697
Total overdues	328113	170197	284115	782425

13. Risk Fund

The creation of risk fund was withdrawn with effect from 1.9.96. At present there is no amount outstanding under Risk Fund.

14. Comprehensive Crop Insurance Scheme

The Bank has been implementing the comprehensive crop insurance scheme through its branches and Farmers Service Societies since 1985. The Bank has submitted 928 declarations covering 40651 farmers during Kharif 99 season insuring a sum of Rs. 399600 thousands by remitting a premium of Rs. 3411 thousands to GIC of India during 1999-2000. Government of

India has introduced new Crop Insurance Scheme namely Rashtriya Krishi Bima Yojana or National Agricultural Insurance Scheme (NAIS) with effect from Rabi 1999-2000 in place of present CCIS. As the Government of Andhra Pradesh has not given their consent for the new scheme, the bank has not implemented new scheme for Rabi 1999-2000.

During 1999-2000, the Bank has received insurance claim settlement of Rs. 10900 thousand for Kharif 98 season benefiting 6564 farmers of Cuddapah and Kurnool district covering Groundnut, Sunflower and Paddy crops. Like wise Rs. 1709 was received as insurance claim for Rabi 1998-99 season from GIC of India benefiting 2 farmers of Kurnool District for Jowar Crop.

15. Write Off Loans

As a part of overall strategy worked out to bring down the level of NPAs, write-off exercises were implemented in respect of irrecoverable loans upto an outstanding limit of Rs. 10000/- (after adjusting CGC claims and deposits), which are considered as bad and doubtful of recovery. This has resulted in eliminating large number of irrecoverable bad and doubtful loan accounts. The loan accounts and amount write off under direct scheme and compromise settlement during the current year and previous year are furnished below.

(Rs. in thousands)

	1998-99		*1999-2000*	
	Accounts	*Amount*	*Accounts*	*Amount*
Written off loans	12363	20458	10373	36432

Chapter—5

Summary and Conclusions

The rural transformation and reconstruction can only be achieved by pumping credit in rural economy. There is no doubt that credit is important and constitutes the key-element in the sphere of almost every economic activity. To improve the rural areas, the banking facilities must bring closer to the small and rural borrowers. To keep this main objective in view, the Regional Rural Banks were established. But there is also the possible danger that Regional Rural Banks would also tend to come under greater political pressures at the local level.

In India, the Reserve Bank of India, the State Bank of India and its associate Banks, 14 Public Sector Commercial Banks and Co-operative Credit Societies, Lead Banks, Regional Rural Banks, Farmers Service Societies, Agricultural Finance Corporation, Agriculture Credit Corporation, Agriculture Refinance Corporation, State Financial Corporation, Small Farmers Development Association, National Small Industries Corporation are the Financial Institutions.

With all these institutions functioning for the rehabilitation and progress of rural communities, there does not appear to be any worth while improvement in the levels of living of the vast masses of village communities. It is no use just going on multiplying banking and financial institutions in rural areas in the name of the Multi-Agency Approach. First, simple and uncomplicated credit structure providing adequate and timely credit at reasonable rates of interest and covering all sections of the community and touching all phases of their economic activities is a 'must' to uplift the rural economy. Secondly, if the rural masses continue to be illiterate, ignorant, apathetic and indifferent the banking and financial institutions in rural areas, would only come to be exploited by the well-to-do sections of the rural community. This would mean that, to enable banking and financial institutions to function properly, rural masses will have to be educated and organised.

Finally, it needs to be emphasised that in the ultimate analyses credit or even credit-rationing may not be the final answer to the problems of poverty in rural areas. As the saying goes, you may take a horse to the pond but you cannot make it drink water. Credit may be rationed with due allotment to the poorer and weaker sections among the rural population. But, what if they do not demand it or cannot make use of it for want of productive opportunities in rural areas. The only way is to stimulate broadbased economic development in rural regions of the country. Naturally, this is primarily the responsibility of the State Government, no doubt, financial and banking institutions can help State Governments in their effort by identifying viable projects, processing them, strengthening field staff and simplifying their procedures. To cast themselves in a more ambitious role would certainly end in frustration.

There is no doubt that credit is important and constitutes the key-element in the share of almost every economic activity. Credit plays a vital role in agricultural progress. Indian rural people do not have funds of their own to carry out their agricultural operations, ranging from ploughing to marketing of the produce. They have not been able to secure adequate and cheap finance for their seasonal agricultural operations or for making permanent improvements to land.

To bring about the overall development in the rural areas, financial assistance to the rural poor particularly institutional assistance needs boosting. Small and marginal farmers constitute bulk of the rural population; these categories are not in a position to improve their economic conditions and income levels because of the low investment capacity. Providing credit may lead to create employment and income and may lead to the agricultural development and pave the way for achieving the desired objective of rural development. If required finance is not available out of ones own income, then one is forced to seek external source of finance i.e., credit. Rural population mainly constitute agricultural producers tenant cultivators, village artisans, land less labour etc., all these categories most of the times are in need of credit.

There is no doubt that the banking system has made phenomenal progress, especially since the nationalisation of the 14 major Commercial Banks in 1969. Great progress has been recorded both in the spheres of branch expansion and functional diversification. It may also be admitted that the Indian Commercial Banking System continues to suffer yet from many serious deficiencies, shortcomings, and inadequacies.

It is still true that with all the progress recorded by Commercial Banking in rural areas, the poor households in rural areas hardly get any finance from this institutional source, which for all practical purposes, does not exist for these poor sections of the rural community. Small and marginal farmers and the poor rural households continue to depend as yet on non-institutional sources of finance (such as agricultural and professional moneylenders, traders and relatives and friends) even for productive enterprises and efforts. Under these circumstances, the Government seriously thought of establishing the Regional Rural Banks.

On the recommendations of a working group, the Regional Rural Banks were started functioning from 1975. The Regional Rural Banks were set up mainly with a view to develop the rural economy by providing credit and other facilities for the purpose of development of agriculture, trade, commerce, industry and other productive activities in the rural areas particularly to the small and marginal farmers, agricultural labourers, artisans and small entrepreneurs.

Bibliography

Patel, A.D. and Singh, S.B., *Small Farmers and Bank Borrowings*. The Banker, Vol. XXVI, No. 5, July, 1979.

Mohan, N., *Service Co-operatives and Small Farmer*, Rural India, 55(9) September, 1972.

Malyadri, P., *Financing Pig Farming—A Study*. Kurukshetra, Vol. XXXVII No. 3, December, 1988.

Nagabhushana Rao, E. and Krishna Murthy, B., *Five Years of Regional Rural Banks*. Kurukshetra, Vol. XXIX No. 8, January 16, 1981.

Vasan Anand Kumar, *Performance of Regional Rural Banks*. Kurukkshetra, Vol. XXXVI no. 8, May, 1988.

Tewari Amitabh, *Rural Oriented Banking in India*. Southern Economist, 21(6), 15 July, 1982.

Sujana Kumari, J., *The Role of Sree Anantha Grameena Bank in a Drought Prone District*. M. Phil., Thesis, S.K. University, Anantapur, 1984.

Subba Rao, K., *Credit to Farmers Who Benefits*. Kurukshetra, Vol. XXVII, No. 1, October, 1979.

Naresh Kumar, *How Banks help in Rural Development*. Kurukshetra, 30(17),1 June, 1982.

Pai Panandivar, V.A., *Regional Rural Banks*. Economic Times (Supplement), 26 June, 1982.

Pate, V.C., *Problems of Bank Branches in Rural Areas*. Eastern Economist, December, 27th, 1968.

Ramola, K.S. and Negi, K.S., *Regional Rural Banks and Rural Development—A Case Study*. Yojana, July 15, 1991.

Surun, L.L., *Role of Co-operative Credit Societies and Commercial Banks*. Khadi Gramodyog, 14(7), April, 1967.

Radha Raman Singh, *Regional Rural Banks and the Rural Poor*. Kurukshetra, Vol. XXXI, No. 11, February 16, 1983.

Ramappa, P., *A Study of Overdues in Regional Rural Banks—with Special Reference to Sree Anantha Grameena Bank*. M.Phil., Thesis, S.K. University, Anantapur, 1982.

Wali, N.M.K., *How Credit Co-operative Fail to Reach the Rural Poor*. Kurukshetra, Vol. XXVIII, No. 8, June, 1980.

Naidu, N.C.B., *Rural Banking—Some Issues*. The Economic Studies, Vol. 19, No. 1, September, 30, 1978.

Naresh Kumar, *Regional Rural Banks Helps Rural Development*. The Maharashtra Co-operative Quarterly, Vol IXVI, No. 2, October, 1982.

Pattak, S.M., *Institutional Credit for Agriculture*. Indian Journal of Agricultural Economics, Vol. XXVII, No. 2, April-June, 1972.

Velayudham, T.K. and Sankaranarayanan, *Regional Rural Banks and Rural Credit*. Economic and Political Weekly, September, 22, 1990.

Kodandaram Naidu, L., *Rural Banking in Andhra Pradesh*. Paper presented to the National Seminar on Bank Finance and Rural Development, 7th and 8th April, 1984.

Natarajan, B., *Regional Rural Banks for Integrated Rural Development*. Swarajya, 21(7),14 August, 1976.

Panda Prabhakar, *Rural Development. Role of Banks Rural India,* 44(8), August, 1981.

Ramana Murthy, D.V., *Regional Rural Bank—An Assessment of Performance*. Southern Economist, 16(7), 1 August, 1977.

Ratanlal Gupta, *What Rural Banks Need To Do?* The Economic Studies, Vol. 16, No. 34, September-October, 1975.

Samanta, R.K., *Attitude Towards Nationalised Banks and Repayment of Agricultural Credit Uses*. Indian Co-operative Review, Vol. XXI, No. 4, April 1984.

Satyasundaram, I., *Problems Facing By Regional Rural Banks*. Paper presented at the Seminar on *Changing Trends in Development Banking*, Conducted by the Department of Commerce, Andhra University, Waltair, 1982.

Mukherjee, P., *Banks and Rural Development*. Khadi Gramodyog, 23(3), 1976.

Dr. Nadem Mohsin and Raghunath Jha, *Regional Rural Banks and IRDP*. Yojana, July 16-31, 1987.

Thingalaya, N.K., *The Regional Rural Banks and Agriculture*, Commerce, 139(3577) 1979.

Tripathi, S.D., *Integrated Approach to Rural Banking*. Eastern Economist, Vol. 65, No. 8, 1976.

Sujit Sikidar, *Problems of Institutional Finance in Hill Areas*. Kurukshetra, Vol. XXXVII, No. 3, Dec. 1988.

Agarwal, R.N., *Rural Banking in India*. Oxford and I.B.H. Publishers, New Delhi.

Charanjit Chanana, *Agricultural Finance in India—Role of Commercial Banks*. Marketing and Research Bureau, New Delhi, 1969.

Ghosh, B.B., *Problems of Rural Credit in India*, Calcutta, 1948.

Nanavathi, M.B. and Anjaria, J.J., *The Indian Rural Problems*. Indian Society of Agricultural Economics, Bombay, 1976.

Reserve Bank of India, *Studies in Agricultural Credit*, 1970.

Savaraiah, G. and Nirmala Mani, *Role of Lead Bank—A Case Study.* Yojana, Vol. 33, No. 6, April 11-15, 1989.

Sharma, K.K., *Role of Regional Rural Banks.* Southern Economist, 14(21), March 1, 1976.

Siva Prasad, D., *Regional Rural Banks.* Journal of Rural Development, May, 1983.

Subash J. Rele, *Rural Banking—Some Special Problems.* Khadi Gramodyog, Vol. 21, No. 8, May, 1975.

Sharada, H.M., *Study of the Regional Rural Banks.* Lok Udyog, 14(3), June, 1980.

Srivastava, R.N., *Impact of Champaram Kshtriya Grameena Bank on Rural Economy.* Economic Affairs, Vol. 26, No. 1, 1981.

Paipanandiker and Mehta, N.C., *Rural Banking.* Bombay National Institute of Bank Management, 1974.

Nakkiran, S., *Agricultural Financing and Rural Banking in India.* Rainbow Publication, Coimbatore, 1980.

Agarwal, R.K., *Evaluation of the Working of Regional Rural Banks.* Mittal Publications, New Delhi, 1991.

Alak Ghosh, *Role of Regional Rural Banks.* The Economic Studies, Vol. 17, No. 1, July, 1976.

Batra, J.D., *Rural Banks for the Rural Poor.* Kurukshetra, 26(2), 16 October, 1977.

Bhabatosh Dutta, *Planning for Rural Banks.* Economic and Political Weekly, Vol. 11, No. 35, August 27th, 1977.

Ganguti, A.K., *Rural Banking.* Margin, Vol. 9, No. 2, January, 1977.

Jagadish Prasad and Sunil Kumar, *Role of Regional Rural Banks.* Kurukshetra, Vol. XXXIII, No. 14, May, 1985.

Venkata Reddy, K., *Rural Development in India—Poverty and Development.* Himalaya Publishing House, Bombay, 1987.

REPORTS

Reserve Bank of India, *Regional Rural Banks Act of 1976*.

Andhra Pradesh Government, *Five Year Plan Reports and Statistical Abstracts*.

Reserve Bank of India, Report of the *Central Banking Enquiry Committee, 1931*.

Report of All India Rural Credit Review Committee, Chairman, D. Venkatappaiah, Bombay, 1969.

Report of the Review Committee on Regional Rural Banks, Dantwala Committee, Bombay, 1977.

Index